Ballet
in Moscow Today

by

Hélène Bellew

NEW YORK GRAPHIC SOCIETY

GREENWICH, CONNECTICUT, U.S.A.

ⓒ New York Graphic Society, Greenwich,
Connecticut U.S.A.
This book is being published in England
by Thames and Hudson Ltd. London.
Printed in Italy by Amilcare Pizzi S.p.A. - Milan

CONTENTS

To
Galina Ulanova and Margot Fonteyn, Prime Ballerine
Assolute, devoted to and safeguarding one tradition

Ballet in Moscow Today

It was with the coming of Serge Diaghilev to Western Europe shortly before the first World War and his surrounding himself with brilliant collaborators in the fields of choreography, music and stage décor that the words *Russian Ballet* were established as an international term. Before then there had been Ballet in Denmark, Ballet in Italy, Ballet in France, Ballet in Sweden and Ballet in Russia, but with the arrival of Diaghilev and his company a noun became an adjective and eventually almost a superlative to be associated with all that was best—the peak—in so-called *classical* dancing. Diaghilev brought with him tradition and standards, devoting his genius to their development and improvement. In addition, and equally if not more importantly, he brought with him Michael Fokine to revolutionize existing choreographic conceptions.

Russian Ballet spelled collaboration between the most outstanding dancers, the most progressive and inventive choreographers, the most brilliant musicians and the most creative painters.

After the death of Diaghilev in 1929 and the disbanding of his company it appeared for a while that there would be no one to carry on where he left off.

But in 1932, René Blum with Colonel W. de Basil regrouped the company with Massine, Balanchine, Danilova, Woizikowsky and others and a new era began. The backbone was composed of former members of the Diaghilev company but young dancers who had never seen Russia and talented newcomers of various origins were added. For décor and music Diaghilev had selected Picasso, Rouault, Pevsner, Gabo Bakst, Benois, Ravel, de Falla, Satie, Stravinsky, and Auric. Blum and de Basil chose Miró, Masson, Bérard, Tchaikowsky, Berlioz, Bizet and Brahms —the term *Russian Ballet* regained its full meaning.

It is unnecessary to recount the fortunes both good and ill which followed the de Basil and other companies which sprang up in France, U.S.A., England and elsewhere between 1932 and today.

It is sufficient perhaps to recall that in spite of its very British character and the world renown won by the Covent Garden-Sadlers Wells Company and the successes of "National" companies, such as the New York City Ballet, it is not uncommon still to hear members of their audiences refer to them as *Russian Ballet*.

But even before the death of Diaghilev, in fact shortly after the last dancers—Danilova, Balanchine, Lifar amongst them—had arrived from Russia in the mid-twenties to join him, questions arose in the minds of all *balletomanes* in the Western World:

What of the *Russian* Russian Ballet? Had it maintained its traditions? Had it developed and if so in which direction?

Contradictory news, or rather rumours, filtered through from Moscow and Leningrad at rare intervals—Ballet had not progressed. It was the best in the world! It was used as a purely political propaganda instrument. The dancers were inferior but the choreographers brilliant! The dancers were outstanding but the choreographers concentrated solely on acrobatics!

What was the truth? Few people from the West with a knowledge of Ballet penetrated the so-called *Iron-Curtain* in the period between the two wars. Certainly no one intimately connected with the production of Ballet. It is true that Fokine paid a brief visit and Isadora Duncan lived some years in the Soviet Union, but Fokine reported little or nothing and Isadora Duncan's interest was her own style of dance and she gave the outside world no real appraisal of the conditions she found.

With the recent war a few *balletomanes* found themselves in the Soviet Union for brief stays, but war conditions prevailed and the fundamental questions remained unanswered. What then in reality is to be found? An Aladdin's Cave or Mother Hubbard's cupboard?

The answer however is not as simple as that.

Certainly Soviet Ballet today resembles in no way Mother Hubbard's cupboard and it comes very close to Aladdin's Cave. But there are some bare areas in the corners and, in spite of the sparkling jewels it contains, a certain amount of dust has been allowed to remain undisturbed too long.

Firstly it should be stated that no country in the Western World posses or has ever possessed such a galaxy of brilliant dancers as exists today in the Soviet Union. And when one speaks of Ballet in the Soviet Union one for all intents and purposes refers to the Bolshoi Theatre Company in Moscow. In spite of its long history and jealously guarded traditions, the Leningrad Company today takes second place to its sister organisation which, being located in the political capital of the U.S.S.R., receives much more official attention and patronage. The Stanislavsky Theatre in Moscow is the home of a well disciplined and talented company possessing a number of brilliant dancers but its general standard is not to be compared with that of the Bolshoi.

Nowhere today are productions so spectacular or on such a grand scale as at the Bolshoi and never—I suspect not even in the days of Diaghilev— has so much been spent on the training of dancers and the staging of productions.

Apart from the vast financial resources so obviously placed at its disposal, the Bolshoi Company possesses for its productions a stage so vast that those of most Western theatres are dwarfed by comparison. The Covent Garden Opera House stage, generally considered large, for example, is only one third as deep and has a proscenium hardly more than half as high. It is not surprising therefore that Moscow audiences accept as normal a stage occupied by more than one hundred dancers, an equal number of musicians in elaborate costumes, supplementing the full symphony orchestra in the pit and scores of extras, not to mention a galloping horse or two.

But for we Western European theatre-goers, who have witnessed change and development in all aspects of Theatre since the early years of the century, to visit the Bolshoi is to step back into another epoch. It is a shock to discover that the whole vast field of ballet production has been almost completely untouched since the departure of Diaghilev. Sitting watching this company, who as dancers and artists have no equals in the world today, one wonders how the spirit of twentieth century experimentation and invention could have passed by the many choreographers and producers of this huge organisation.

Like the Sleeping Princess herself, the Bolshoi company has kept its beauty but been asleep—not for a century but a good forty to fifty years. Aurora, sleeping in her palace, was guarded by a vast barrier of forest growth and the evil followers of Karabos. Soviet choreographers and producers have been surrounded by an equally impregnable screen—*isolation*. No modern influence has succeeded in penetrating this most unyielding of all "curtains". All the ballets performed are like perfectly kept period pieces, jealously preserved within their heavy, lavishly ornamented, nineteenth century frames.

When Fokine left his native Russia to join Diaghilev, he left behind him a tradition—a great tradition owing most perhaps to Petipa but one in danger of stagnation. Fokine realised this peril and, under the inspiring guidance of Diaghilev, set about revolutionising existing conceptions of the roles of choreography, décor, costume, music and "theme".

He had already made known his ideas for ballet reform to the responsible authorities in St Petersburg, but little or no heed had been paid them. He had insisted, and he was to do so until the end of his days, that ballet must be a harmonious marriage between music, painting and dance movement, and to achieve this there must be the closest collaboration between musicians, painters and choreographers.

With this guiding principle ever in his mind, he created such master-pieces as *Les Sylphides, Petrouchka, Shéhérazade, l'Oiseau de Feu* and *Carnaval*, and it was this principle that he bequeathed to his choreographic heirs, Massine and Balanchine, enabling them to make the "revolution" complete.

A comparison not too far astray might be: Petipa, Fokine, Massine and Balanchine—Impressionism, Cézanne, Cubism and Abstract art. But this transition, in both choreography and painting, has passed, if not unnoticed, certainly unheeded in the U.S.S.R.

Nothing of Fokine remains except *Chopiniana* and this is only occasionally presented as a vehicle to display the abilities of graduation classes in the Leningrad school.

Only three "modern" composers have been utilised—Prokofiev, Shostakovitch and Khachaturyan. Prokofiev produced the scores for *Romeo and Juliet, Cinderella* and *the Stone Flower*. Shostakovitch wrote the music for *the Golden Age* and *the Bright Stream*. Neither are presented today. Khachaturyan composed *the Prisoner* which is also no longer performed.

Far from the achievement of an equal partnership between musician, painter and choreographer there has been allowed to continue the old practice of independence and inequality. A fourth and dominating factor has also entered—the librettist. In the Western world the libretto is generally merely a starting point—an inspiration—for the choreographer who does with it what he will. In the U.S.S.R. it completely dominates him. He must arrange his choreography so that no detail, however small, shall be omitted or not fully understood by his audience. Costumes and décor must be equally detailed.

There was a period—now happily almost passed — when the stress was on librettos strongly political in character. However, the insistance on literary content is still maintained. An example is *Swan Lake* now being presented in its seventh version. I was informed in Moscow that yet another rewriting is to be made to make the story more comprehensible to the audience.

For décor, producers have remained faithful for the most part to traditional, highly realistic, constructed "opera" sets—incredibly spectacular and magnificent, but hardly designed to avoid lack of balance between decoration and choreography.

It seems a paradox indeed that in the U.S.S.R., a land where revolution is the key word, that a nineteenth century imported tradition—for Petipa was born in Marseilles and the constructed scenery and painted cloths used in Moscow productions today have no link with traditional Russian art—has been so jealously guarded against all change while outside its borders Russian born directors, choreographers, painters and musicians have succeeded in eliminating the last vestiges of conservatism.

It is difficult in the extreme to equate this respect for the academic within the walls of the Bolshoi Theatre with the spirit of research and experiment that exists elsewhere throughout the country. It seems strange that the influence of avant-garde, Russian born choreographers and artists, who in their work express the very spirit of the twentieth century, should be neglected for an ultra conservative foreign tradition of a past era.

But perhaps, with the changes in attitude already to be noticed in other spheres, a new approach to the aesthetics of ballet production can be expected in the not too distant future.

In the choreography of Fokine, Massine and Balanchine there is much inspiration to be drawn and in the painting of Malevitch, Sonia Delaunay, Chagall, Kandinsky, Gontcharova and Larionov, to name but a few, there is native tradition and the true spirit of revolution. However if, in the U.S.S.R., it is the librettist who calls the tune and the scenic designer who strives to dazzle the audience with mammoth sized settings and bewildering stage mechanics, the Soviet choreographer has not, as one might have expected and perhaps justified, resorted to the employment of choreographic "fireworks" to gain attention. In fact I know of no company which pays less attention to "acrobatics" than the Bolshoi.

In the choreography of R. Zakharov (*The Fountain of Bakhchisarai, The Bronze Horseman, Cinderella*), L. M. Lavrovsky (*Romeo and Juliet, Fadetta*), V. M. Chaboukiani (*Laurencia*) and V. Vainonen (*Flames of Paris, Mirandolina*), there is much sensitivity and imagination and although it is often obscured almost completely by scenery, costume and other story-telling devices, not one of has them sought compensation by utilising excessive turns or other acrobatic tricks.

Indeed their choreography has a quality of understatement which could well be noted by some Western choreographers.

In *The Fountain of Bakhchisarai*, for example, Zakharov has introduced a series of "lifts" for the Khan Girei and Maria which for pure plastic beauty and meaning are unsurpassed anywhere in the world today. With a slight emphasis, their inventiveness and intricacies could be revealed to gain acclaim from the audience which, in Moscow as much as elsewhere, is ever-ready to applaud the spectacular.

In the Western world ballerinas are too often tempted and encouraged by choreographers to attract this type of easy applause. Given entrances on to almost empty stages, they frequently make them with the over confidence and exaggeration of the circus to demonstrate the complexity of the choreography and their individual technical brilliance.

This attitude is taboo in Moscow and the "bravura" dancer the very rare exception.

The Dancers

Headed by the almost legendary Ulanova, the Bolshoi Company numbers more than two hundred dancers and presents a current repertoire of fifteen ballets.

Much has been claimed for Ulanova both abroad and in the Soviet Union where, in the hearts and minds of people in all walks of life, she has been elevated to the position almost of a deity.

Numerous books have been written about her and all are unanimous that she is the greatest ballerina of this decade.

She is a dancer with an indescribable quality, her performances being the result of a highly sensitive personality, impeccable technique and an uncanny talent for changing her whole being according to her conception of her rôles. Her intellectual approach to both movement and music is also a large factor of her phenomenal success.

In class she is a being dedicated to her art and in some strange way she gives the onlooker the feeling of watching a devoted believer at prayer. It is possible that her name is more frequently on the lips of the average Soviet citizen than that of any living politician, writer or artist. She has been showered with official honours and although she now appears less and less on the stage, no other ballerina has been able to fill her place in the hearts of the public.

Like so many leading dancers of the Bolshoi—amongst them Semyonova, Preobrazhenski and Yermolaev—Ulanova came originally from the Leningrad School, graduating in 1928 with Natalie Dudinskaya. It is only necessary to see her in class, which she attends as regularly and with as much seriousness as the youngest member of the Company, to recognise her immediately as a Leningrad-trained ballerina.

Western dancers who have had the advantage of training with Lubov Egorova, Alexandre Volinine, Preobrajenskaia or other Russian teachers, will know what I mean—the strictly classical so-called "Italian" School demanding high technical brilliance, perfection and virtuosity which has been the hall-mark of the Leningrad School since the late XIXth century.

This preoccupation with precision and "fireworks" is still much appreciated and maintained in Leningrad while, in Moscow the stress has always been on dramatic feeling and a free flowing expressive line. However, in recent years a general blending of the two has been achieved at the Bolshoi where many of the teachers, and a great number of the leading dancers, are from Leningrad.

The rigidity of the Leningrad *port de bras* and the free flowing line and expressive individual arm and body movements of the Moscow teaching are complementing each other to perfection, softening the classical stiffness of the first and controlling the abandon of the latter, resulting in a pure poetic movement which gives grace and poise to the smallest talent—the most difficult technical feats are performed effortlessly and expressively, rather than as monotonously executed *tours de force*.

Ulanova on stage combines all that is expressively possible with an incredible technique so effortless that it is never obvious to the eye. Her rôles are never a sequence of dances performed in front of the spectator, but a series of living personalities. You live every moment of tragedy with her Maria in *The Fountain of Bakhchisarai* and her Giselle. You dream and share every emotion with her Juliet and experience all the pathos and rapture of her Cinderella.

Genius may be too great a term to describe her infinite artistry, but only two other dancers, to my knowledge, have the right to the same claim to greatness—Thamar Karsavina and Olga Spessiva.

Her most famous rôles are perhaps Juliet in *Romeo and Juliet*, Maria in *The Fountain of Bakhchisarai* and *Giselle*, which history states has two initial choreographers—Coralli for the main ballet and Perrot who composed all the scenes and dances for his wife Carlotta Grisi, the originator of the rôle of Giselle.

However, not only does Ulanova excel in these more romantic rôles, but her Odette-Odile in *Swan Lake* which she interpreted in 1929 for the first time in Leningrad after being a member of the company for only one year, is, with her Aurora in *The Sleeping Beauty* and Raimonda, one of her most renowned successes.

Ulanova herself gives much importance to her rôle of Tao Hoa in *The Red Poppy*—a ballet no longer included in the Bolshoi repertoire but still performed occasionally in Leningrad. In spite of a rather beautifully arranged *pas de deux* between Tao Hoa and Ma-Li-Chen, the young coolie, in the second act, this ballet, overcharged with political content, is an outstanding proof of how the inclusion of political propaganda in a work of art results in failure both aesthetically and politically. *The Red Poppy* is, fortunately for the integrity and progress of Soviet ballet, the last remaining example of extreme political domination.

Ulanova recently has not been free from ill health and, in spite of her incredible technical skill and dramatic qualities, the day of her retirement is drawing near. When this ill-fated moment arrives there will be sadness not only amongst ballet lovers throughout the world, but also in the hearts of all people throughout the Soviet Union. It is impossible to indicate the degree of affection with which she is held by her countrymen.

All dancers who come after her will be faced inevitably by audiences who will compare every step and gesture with those of their beloved Ulanova. This, of course, is the fate of all dancers who follow an "idol", but it can be said without hesitation that there exists already at the Bolshoi a number of ballerinas of the Ulanova mould.

Her departure, sad as it can only be, will have the compensation of giving others opportunities for which they have long been ready and which, because of their rare abilities, they richly deserve.

Olga Lepechinskaya

Olga Lepechinskaya who, with Maya Plisetskaya, fills second position after Ulanova in the company, is a completely different dancer. Although she graduated with the title of *première danseuse*, she is not a prima ballerina in the sense we give the term in the West. Her style is *demi-caractère* and, although this term is not used in Russia, she is the very essence of what it covers. One of the strongest technicians in the U.S.S.R. today, her elevation is remarkable and her turns brilliant, absolutely sure, and finished with almost masculine force. However, rather studied, nervous movements of arms and head with an accompanying lack of grace and poise detract from many of her performances. Her *attitudes* and *arabesques* are frequently void of line and fluency as she attempts to accomplish everything with bravura. The Moscow public, it must be admitted, respond enthusiastically to this type of studied brilliance and showmanship.

Her performances, in spite of her brilliant technique and vivacity, are liable to leave the true ballet-lover restive and disappointed.

As Kitri in *Don Quixote*, a rôle created in 1871 by Andreyanova at the Marinsky, she has her best vehicle for her particular type of purely technical dancing. Highly rated by her public and popular among her colleagues, she is a valuable ballerina to the company, technically capable of dancing any rôle in the repertoire.

Maya Plisetskaya

Maya Plisetskaya is one of the most "finished" dancers at the Bolshoi. Her very appearance on stage is exciting and it is evident immediately that here is a truly great ballerina.

Her every movement has meaning, her technique is immaculate and physically she is slender, well proportioned and very beautiful. She has combined a precise, faultless technique with the flowing movements of the Moscow school to perfection. This, with a rare elevation—a family inheritance, as she is a niece of Zulamith and Asaf Messerer,—an infinite femininity, and highly developed lyrical and romantic qualities, makes her one of the most gifted ballerinas of today.

Possessing elegant long limbs, soft and lovely arms—the most beautiful since Spessiva—her *port de bras* and every slightest movement of her hands are always part of the music. Her Aurora, in *The Sleeping Beauty*, is a superb performance. In *adage* work she is excellent and always in perfect unison with her partner.

A great deal of the original Petipa choreography has been changed in the current production and one is inclined to feel the absence of Petipa more in the Rose adagio than in the other well-known *variations*. However, Plisetskaya gives such warmth and youthful femininity to her dance with her four suitors that even the Rose adagio in its old form is not missed.

Odette-Odile in *Swan Lake* is perhaps her best rôle to date. Her authority, elegance and immaculate style give the perfect illusion of the Swan Princess. In her interpretation of the part of Odile she makes the perfect contrast between the vicious gaiety and mischievousness of the daughter of the evil genius and the tender romantic qualities of the Swan Princess.

Possessing full command of her stage, she performs all technical feats with equal ease and brilliance, never departing from the true mood of her rôle. Plisetskaya is equally at home in character work. The rôle of Zarema in *The Fountain of Bakhchisarai* gives her full opportunity to reveal her dramatic abilities and demonstrate her remarkable versatility as an artist.

It is to be hoped that one day she will be given the rôles of Juliet in *Romeo and Juliet* and Maria in *The Fountain of Bakhchirasai*. She would give the infinite feeling and tenderness necessary to both.

Raissa Struchkova

Raissa Struchkova is a beautifully made dancer with physically everything in her favour. A young ballerina of great technical knowledge, who has been given every chance to develop, she dances most of Ulanova's rôles. Her technique is brilliant but sometimes tends to be more brittle than truly graceful in purely classical rôles. As Aurora in *The Sleeping Beauty*, she lacks the warmth and femininity which she expresses as Maria in *The Fountain of Bakhchisarai* and as Juliet in *Romeo and Juliet*. As *Aurora* her arm movements are liable to be too studied and lacking in expression. Her hands, often rigid in a set pose, are liable to mar her otherwise fluent line.

She has long, well formed legs and beautifully moulded neck and shoulders. She has an excellent sense of line and in partner work she excels. Her *attitudes* in supported *adage* are of rare perfection. Her line is poetic and of infinite grace whilst her every "lift" is expressive and seemingly effortless.

Her Maria in *The Fountain of Bakhchisarai* is one of her best performances. In the first act she gives great expression to her *variations* with Vatslav her fiancé and, in a beautifully arranged *pas de deux,* she demonstrates how well the dancers of the Bolshoi company know how to walk and run naturally on stage—avoiding at all times the stilted "ballerina walk" unfortunately accepted in most Western Ballet companies.

In the third act her tragic duet with the Khan Girei is one of the most moving moments of the ballet but in her scene with Zarema she rather fails to express the depth of her sorrow. However, her "dream" of her past happiness at home with her father and her lover is poetically and beautifully portrayed. Here she finds the true expression so needed throughout this ballet but in her final death scene she does not equal the dramatic talent of Plisetskaya in conveying the depth of the tragedy. There is a quality of understatement in many of Struchkova's interpretations which gives a feeling of cool beauty and poise rather than emotional depth. But she is nevertheless capable of expressing strong dramatic emotions as in the scene when Juliet's father announces her approaching marriage to Paris. Her hurried visit to Friar Laurence (Act III, Scene 2) gives her another opportunity for dramatic expression which she fulfils admirably, while she makes the return to her room, where her father and mother await her anxiously, a scene of extreme tension. Here she has perhaps her greatest acting moments. Her pretence of submitting to her father's will and her apathetic dance with Paris are intensely moving as is also her frenzied solo from the taking of the potion to her final fall upon her bed.

A. Yermolaev

One of the most famed artists at the Bolshoi today, Yermolaev was a pupil of Vaganova. Possessing a virtuoso technique, his elevation at its best is approaching the legendary *ballon* of Nijinsky.

He is to be seen at his best as Albrecht in *Giselle* and as Tybalt in *Romeo and Juliet*. To both these rôles he brings, in addition to his wide technical abilities, an excellent histrionic sense and style.

V. Preobrazhenski

A self-effacing and truly great partner, he now appears less frequently than in previous years. Although getting physically a little heavy for purely classical rôles, he possesses a noble appearance and is the perfect support for his ballerina.

In *The Fountain of Bakhchisarai* as Vatslav, he partners Maria with perfection but fails on occasions to give a finished rendering of his own solos.

Y. Kondratov

A virile brilliant dancer with excellent technique although inclined to carelessness and flamboyance, Kondratov is one of the most valuable dancers in the company. He is an excellent partner and manages his ballerina, if not always with care in difficult movements, with the experience and *savoir faire* which only the born dancer-partner possesses. The lack of discipline he shows on occasions is regrettable and completely unnecessary in one so talented and experienced.

His performance in *Laurencia* demonstrates at once his showmanship, technique and excellence as a partner. As Basil in *Don Quixote* he is outstanding but in the final *grand pas de deux* and subsequent solos and coda he sometimes neglects the finish which adds to this spectacular sequence an unnecessary and out of place touch of the circus.

S. Korèn

A dancer of extreme lightness and elegance, he excels in character parts. In *Romeo and Juliet* as Mercutio his outstanding dramatic abilities are shown to the full. In the death scene after the duel with Tybalt he gives a truly masterful performance.

A. Lapauri

This magnificent partner and sensitive artist is worth his weight in gold to any ballet company. With his strong technique, great musicality, striking appearance, commanding presence, expressiveness and finesse, I believe there is no one to surpass him as an artist among his fellow *premiers danseurs*. Nor is there anyone who can "present" his ballerina with such unselfishness and effect.

His work in both supported *adage* and straight partnering is ideal in all respects. Every lift of his partner becomes an integral part of the music, charged with meaning and void of any feeling of acrobatics. His performance as the Khan Girei in *The Fountain of Bakhchisarai* is superb, demanding full utilisation of all his rare talents as both partner and dramatic artist.

It is to be regretted greatly that when the company goes on tour the dimensions of Western stages will prevent this spectacular ballet being presented in its original settings and with the Bolshoi's full male *corps de ballet*. In the world repertoire of ballet there exists nothing to compete with the fiery dance of Nur Ali and his warriors (Act IV) for colour, abandon and masculine virility. Fokine's famous dances of the Polovtsian warriors from *Prince Igor* is a stately minuet compared to this scene as presented in Moscow.

Lapauri is equally outstanding as Paris in *Romeo and Juliet* and as

Don Fernan in *Laurencia* but *The Fountain of Bakhchisarai* gives him wider scope to display his unique abilities. In *Laurencia* (Act I, Scene 2), he achieves moments of high lyrical as well as dramatic quality in the *pas de deux* which is one of the most moving passages in the choreography of this ballet.

R. Karelskaya

The poise and control of this beautiful dancer make her ideal for all classical rôles. Her expressive arms and pure classical line are accompanied by a flawless technique, elegance and great musicality.

The Lilac Fairy in *The Sleeping Beauty* suits her to perfection. Her interpretation of this rôle is one of extreme tenderness and technically her performance leaves nothing to be desired.

N. Chorokova

Chorokova is one of the most graceful dancers at the Bolshoi, possessing true poetic grace and poise, beautiful arms, expressive limbs and great musicality.

Although she originally failed to gain entrance to the Bolshoi School at the age of seven, she was accepted eight years later and has proved to be a great asset to the company. Like so many brilliant dancers in the company, she is still waiting an opportunity to show her full capabilities in a really major rôle.

The general policy of the company of presenting full-length, four act ballets in which major parts are given to only two or three dancers results in dancers like Chorokova, who would be able immediately to take their place at the head of many Western companies, having to remain in minor positions too long.

In the *pas de trois* in *Swan Lake* she is brilliant and her performance as the actress Mirelle in *Flames of Paris* allows her to demonstrate her great versatility. Always a poised and truly graceful dancer, her variation *à la camargo* in the ballet sequence at the ball at Versailles in *Flames of Paris* (Act II) is a memorable performance. In this rôle also she demonstrates her highly developed lyrical and dramatic qualities.

L. Cherkassova

A taller dancer than the average, she is full blooded rather than subtle in her interpretations.

She has an amazing *elevation* and a beautiful technique but she does not always use it with care. Her *ballon* is exceptional and she fills all her rôles with the joy of dancing.

Her interpretation of the friend of Juliet in *Romeo and Juliet* is a portrayal of a full-blown Venetian beauty possessing complete confidence in her right to acclaim from her suitors.

In purely classical rôles she sometimes gives a feeling of too much energy which tends to detract from their classical mood. She is a ballerina possessing a strong individuality and exuberant enthusiasm for her vocation. One never wishes for another dancer when watching her in a rôle.

Her performance as Zarema in *The Fountain of Bakhchisarai* is charged with meaning and she expresses to perfection both her joy at the return of the Khan Girei and her uncontrollable jealousy of her new rival Maria.

M. Gotlieb

A ballerina with great charm and flawless execution in *demi-caractère* rôles but yet to develop fully from the histrionic point of view, she is definitely one of the most pleasing and polished dancers in the company.

Like Struchkova, she possesses a flawless technique which allows her to perform the most difficult solos with complete absence of visible strain or effort.

The rôle of Jeanne in *Flames of Paris* suits her to perfection but in purely classical rôles such as the Diamond Fairy in *The Sleeping Beauty* she fails to give the sparkle which her technical excellence should allow her to convey to the full.

As Pascuala in *Laurencia* she has a rôle suiting perfectly her gay personality and she executes all her solos and *pas de deux* with brilliance. She still has to develop more feeling in the more dramatic scenes with Laurencia. She is also excellent in the *pas de rois* with Laurencia and Jacinta and in the *pas de six* with Lepechinskaya and Bogolubskaya when partnered by Andrianov, Kondratov and Evdokimov.

Y. D. Sekh

An outstanding, elegant dancer with dramatic talent and an accomplished tecnique, exceptional light elevation and forceful personality.

As Mercutio in *Romeo and Juliet* he gives a fine performance in the death scene (Act II, Scene 3).

G. Evdokimov

A very strong classical and character dancer, his rôles vary from purely classical to the savage Nur Ali in *The Fountain of Bakhchisarai*.

He possesses extraordinary virility and musicality. As Nur Ali he gives more colour, excitement and vigorous abandon to this one part than most companies in the West manage to create with their full *corps de ballet* and soloists. His sensitive, expressive miming is of the highest order and while one may first of all think of him in full blooded character rôles, in classical work he has a noble appearance and faultless technique, making him one of the most valuable soloists at the Bolshoi today.

P. M. Andrianov

A young dancer of perfect classical technique and natural noble appearance he stands out in *ensemble* work. His fencing variation in *The Fountain of Bakhchisarai* (Act I) is of such excellence and lightness that this act loses much when he is absent from the rôle.
With Evdokimov in *Laurencia* he is outstanding.

Yuri Zhdanov

Another excellent technician and lyrical soloist, he is a good partner if sometimes limited dramatically.
In *The Fountain of Bakhchisarai* as Vatslov he is ideally cast and dances his variations to perfection, demonstrating his unusual elevation. In *Romeo and Juliet* he sometimes fails to maintain the character of the rôle throughout but in the tender and romantic scenes with Juliet he is the true Romeo, while in the scene of Juliet's funeral he gives a very moving performance accomplishing the difficult choreography without apparent effort. He is also excellent as Albrecht in *Giselle*.

N. Chistova

We shall know much more of Chistova not so very long from now. She is a dancer brimming over with poetic romanticism with every movement of her expressive limbs.
She possesses a beautiful long line and, like most of the other young soloists in the company, he is technically remarkably strong.
Having the necessary romantic appearance and expression, she gives a convincing performance as Parasha in *The Bronze Horseman*. Her solo work is a delight to watch and in *pas de deux* her line is tender and lyrical while her acting ability is strongly developed.
As Princess Florina in *The Sleeping Beauty* she gives a polished performance in the Bluebird *pas de deux*. But, while her *variation* is technically perfect, her interpretation is rather more romantic than we are accustomed to in the West.
However, the choreography of most of the *variations* in this ballet differs greatly from the versions generally presented by companies outside the U.S.S.R. and if one misses sparkle in the Bolshoi *variations* it is due to the new choreographers and not the dancers.

M. Bogolubskaya

A sensitive artist with an exceptionally wide range, her fragile appearance is in contrast to her very positive and expressive movements on stage.
As Jacinta in *Laurencia* she gives an emotionally complete rendering of the ravished girl and maintains her character throughout, accomplishing all the difficult choreography with ease and fluent grace. In the second act she proves herself an exceptional actress as well as a musical and lyrical dancer.

E. Banke

An extremely accomplished dancer, technically and expressively, with a strong personality and a highly developed musical sense.

As Karabos in *The Sleeping Beauty* she always gives an excellent performance. Her entrance in her carriage surrounded by her suite of rats and monsters, her furious variation ending with the curse on Aurora and her scene with the Lilac fairy are all so embued with spite and wickedness that she appears to be the very incarnation of the fairy Karabos and it is difficult to imagine her in any other rôle. However, she brings the same understanding and artistry to all she does.

J. Tikhorminova

A finely built ballerina, highly musical with a soft feminine appearance and pleasing personality. Her weakness is perhaps a lack of attack which with care could be remedied.

G. Farmanyantz

A strong dancer with a purely classical technique, he excels in *demi-caractère* work, not always, however, being truly convincing in his characterisations.

As Philip in *Flames of Paris*, we see him at his best, his work in the last act with Jeanne possessing great vitality and his variations proving his technical superiority. In *The Sleeping Beauty*, his Bluebird can be as brilliant as it can be careless while his Jester in *Romeo and Juliet* is a rôle he dances to perfection but without always giving sufficient character to the part.

N. Kouznetsov

An artist and dancer possessing great expressive powers, he is a sensitive lyrical partner with an excellent technique.

His Eugène in *The Bronze Horseman* is a thoroughly worked out characterisation showing his talent for dramatic acting. In the scene of the great flood he gives a fine performance impeded only by the fabulous display of scenic mechanics which would "drown" a lesser artist. In Act IV, Scene 2, where he loses his mind, his performance is of an equally high order.

B. Horlov

Another well trained soloist with a noble classical appearance, he is a good partner with excellent elevation and a fine feeling for line and a sensitive ear for music.

As Vatslav in Act I of *The Fountain of Bakhchisarai*, he gives a well danced, poetic performance while his partnering is perfectly timed. His duets with Maria are highlights of Act I.

In the *pas de trois* in *Swan Lake*, he dances and partners his ballerinas with assurance and rare elegance while, as the Troubadour in *Romeo and Juliet* (Act I, Scene 4), he gives a lyrical performance and underlines his excellence as a partner.

J. Gerber

An extremely gifted mime and character dancer with a strong technique and excellent elevation, he has a sympathetic personality and a winning sense of humour.

In *Flames of Paris* his interpretation of Pierre, the brother of Jeanne, is remarkable both for his strong dancing and sense of characterisation.

P. Homutov

An excellent partner possessing a true classical appearance who is also a sensitive mime.

As the actor Antoine Mistral in *Flames of Paris* he appears at his best and in *Romeo and Juliet* as the Troubadour he gives another polished performance.

A. Radunsky

A superb actor-mime whose every interpretation is impeccable. It is a tradition with the Bolshoi company to give equal importance to both acting and dancing parts and to demand equal perfection in their interpretation.

All Radunsky's characterisations are the result of scrupulous preparation and study. As the Master of Ceremonies in *The Sleeping Beauty* he shines, bringing to the rôle artistry and genuine humour, while as Peter the Great in *The Bronze Horseman* he portrays with perfection the true character and manner of the founder of Leningrad. In *The Fountain of Bakhchisarai*, as Maria's father, he gives another brilliant characterisation full of temperament and subtle humour.

E. Kashani

A character dancer with a good technique, he gives a convincing performance as Mengo in *Laurencia* where he shows his acting capabilities as well as proving an excellent partner with a great musical sense.

In *Romeo and Juliet* he is well cast as the Jester.

I. Olenina

An excellent actress and mime—outstanding as Juliet's maid in *Romeo and Juliet*. Every appearance she makes in this ballet is a gem of artistry and characterisation.

Her intelligent understanding of all her rôles and her musicality make her a valuable asset to the choreographer and to the company.

S. Golovkina

A dancer with a strong technique, excelling in purely classical rôles. Emotionally her range is still limited however and consequently in dramatic rôles such as Zarema in *The Fountain of Bakhchisarai* she is yet to give a really complete performance.

20

E. M. Iluchenko

A dancer with a forceful presence and outstanding dramatic qualities, as Juliet's mother in *Romeo and Juliet* she gives a moving characterisation — particularly in the scene with the dead Tybalt (Act II, Scene 3). In *The Sleeping Beauty* she gives a poised and aristocratic performance as the Queen.

N. A. Kapustina

A typically Russian character dancer—dark, vivacious and full of temperament and abandon.

She has dramatic talent and gives an excellent performance of true character dancing when leading the Mazurka and Krakoviak in the first act of *The Fountain of Bakhchisarai*. Her flamengo in *Laurencia* has strength and verve.

T. Tuchina

A "pocket-sized" ballerina with an accomplished, neat technique, brilliant attack and a gay, pronounced personality.

She dances the rôle of Amour in *Flames of Paris* with all the mischievousness and coquetry required, while as one of the little beggars in *Romeo and Juliet* and as Little Red Ridinghood in *The Sleeping Beauty* she proves herself to be a versatile artist.

F. Efremova

An ideal *demi-caractère* dancer and a first rate technician, exceptionally strong on her points, with speed and lightness, she gives a particularly charming performance as Little Red Ridinghood in *The Sleeping Beauty* where she demonstrates all her technical capabilities and introduces all the necessary humour and charm to the rôle.

As one of the little beggars in *Romeo and Juliet* she gives an intelligent and witty characterisation.

I. Makedonskaya

A dancer of refinement with a well developed histrionic sense, she excels as Maria's servant in *The Fountain of Bakhchisarai* (Act III), where she gives a sensitive and sympathetic interpretation. However, she is not so happily cast as Juliet's mother in *Romeo and Juliet*.

Other Dancers

It has been impossible, for reasons of space alone, to list every dancer of talent in this huge company, and to see them all in the rôles in which they excel would have meant remaining in Moscow for many more months than I could afford. Omission therefore is not to be taken as neglect or prejudice on my part.

The Bolshoi School

The Bolshoi school, from which all the company's dancers originate with few exceptions and which supplies new members to the Stanislavsky Company and the theatres in the principal cities throughout the U.S.S.R., is conducted with a scientific thoroughness unknown outside the U.S.S.R. Directed by Boscharnikova, the teachers, headed by Gabovich, include Zulamith and Asaf Messerer and Marina Semyonova.

Pupils enter the school at seven years of age and receive three years general education before starting their first years of ballet training. The girls are not permitted to wear point shoes until the end of this fourth year, by which time they are at least ten years old. (How many small feet are ruined in the West by over-enthusiastic mothers and misguided teachers who permit their youthful owners to stagger "on their toes" before the bone structures are ready and able to support the weight of their bodies!)

During the entire initial year of training, tuition is carefully restricted to the "five positions", *plié en première, à la seconde* and other elementary exercises *à la barre* and to *glissades, assemblés* and *changements*. Then, and only then, with their cherished point shoes they are given their first exercises on point.

With the boys no feat of real technique is attempted until the age of fourteen or fifteen when they start their first steps with *batterie* such as *entrechat trois, brisé volé* and *jeté battu*.

All training for both boys and girls during the early years is executed half time or slow tempo and not until the five positions, centre practice and the *enchaînements* are mastered to perfection are they permitted to start dancing *à tempo*.

The schooling, with stress on precision as well as grace and fluency of line is one of extreme, planned care from the first to graduation year. Exercises both *à la barre* and *au milieu* are from the beginning designed for the large stage of the Bolshoi. Great attention to *développé* and control is given during stretching movements and limbering exercises while during centre practice stress is given to the finish of all combinations. The *allegro* is, when simplified for the beginning classes, given with strict attention to the preparations for elevated steps and on the finishing *chaînés* turns as used in most variations of the classical repertoire. The jumps at the end of class before point work and turns are always simplified but the distance of every leap is prescribed and the *grands jetés en tournant* in a circle are designed with the proportions of the Bolshoi stage ever in mind. The floors in all the class rooms have been constructed so that they slope at the same angle as the Bolshoi stage. Point work is of short duration in most classes and steps are never complicated, main attention being paid to position and "finish". All combinations end with turns *en dehors, en dedans* or with *piqués* and *chaînés* turns *en diagonale*. Some of the more advanced sequences finish on one foot *sur la pointe en attitude* or *en arabesque*.

The adagios *au milieu* are lengthy sequences with stress on extensions, balance and *épaulement,* generally finishing with *grandes pirouettes* or sustained balances *à la seconde* or *en arabesque*.

The piano accompaniment is always improvised by the pianist to suit the teacher's spontaneous arrangements of *adagio, allegro* and point work.

In Asaf Messerer's mixed class for members of the actual Bolshoi company one is able to study the technique of the leading dancers at close range and free from elaborate line-obscuring costumes.

To see Ulanova with her effortless technique alongside the hard working Lepechinskaya at the *barre* and in centre practice gives an immediate understanding of these two artists and their completely opposed styles on stage.

The younger Maya Plisetskaya with her supple body, expressive arms, fluent line and exceptional elevation reveals that she possesses all the qualities of a great prima ballerina.

In class Struchkova has the same distinction as on stage, her brilliant technique and elevation immediately impressing the onlooker.

Among the men Preobrazhenski is distinguished while Kondratov and Zhdanov do not always show themselves to full advantage in class.

At the Leningrad school the same meticulous care and scientific approach is maintained throughout all years of training with particular stress, of course, on strict "Italian" classicism and technical virtuosity.

To say that this school's results are phenomenal seems almost an understatement. Ulanova, Semyonova, Dudinskaya, Preobrazhenski, Yermolaev, Sergeyev, to name but a few, all come from the Leningrad school and at this year's graduation concert in the Kirov Theatre I noticed three truly brilliant dancers — Suleimanova, Antonova and Ivanov — who should be certain ultimately to make world names for themselves. Suleimanova and Antonova need only experience while Ivanov is already, from all points of view, a fully-fledged *premier danseur*.

Appreciation

In addition to the many dancers, choreographers, teachers and administrators who gave me such invaluable assistance and showed me so much kindness during my stay in the U.S.S.R., I wish to thank in particular for their great help and friendship the following; Alexander V. Solodovnikov, Head of the Directorate-General of Theatres and Conservatoriums at the Ministry of Culture of the U.S.S.R., Sergei V. Shashkin, Deputy-Director of the Bolshoi Theatre and P. A. Gussev, Chief Ballet Master, without whose constant aid I would have failed in my mission. Also my deepest thanks are due to Madame Boscharnikova, Directrice of the Bolshoi Ballet School who, with Mikhail Gabovich, welcomed me so graciously at all times and who, without demur, permitted me to disturb strict routine and order.

In Leningrad, my warmest gratitude is due to A.V. Lopukov, Madame Frangopulo, Madame Tatiana Vecheslova and M. Thomson who received me with so much kindness at the Kirov Theatre and School.

I wish also to extend my appreciation to S. Areznikov, Director of the Bolshoi Theatre Literary Department and to the Curator of the Bolshoi Museum who helped me with the problem of photographs for this book. Finally, I am greatly indebted to Igor Stupnikov (Leningrad) and Vladimir Leonidov (Moscow) who shouldered so willingly the burden of my linguistic shortcomings.

H. B.

THE REPERTOIRE

*The Fountain of Bakhchisarai: Act I. N. Chorokova
as Maria and A. Kuznetsov as Vatslav*

The Fountain of Bakhchisarai

Ballet in 4 Acts

MUSIC: B. V. Asafiev

BOOK: N. D. Volkov after the poem of Pushkin

CHOREOGRAPHY: R. Zakharov

First Moscow performance at Bolshoi Theatre 11-6-1936 with V. Vassilieva as Maria

Action of the ballet takes place in Poland and Bakhchisarai during the 18th Century.

Act I: An old park near the castle of the Polish Prince Pototsky. The birthday of his daughter, the young Maria, is being celebrated. From the castle come the strains of an orchestra and, in the park, Maria and her fiancé, Vatslav, are seen dancing oblivious of their surroundings. Hand in hand they go off down the paths of the park.

In the darkness, a scout from the army of the Crimean Khan Girei stealthily enters the park, eluding the guards who pursue him without success.

The guests come out of the castle in a solemn polonaise, led by Maria and her father. The polonaise gives way to a lively Cracovienne. Merriment takes possession of the young people and their elders. Grey-headed, moustached landowners and slender youths, in eager rivalry, make love to the girls.

Vatslav strums on his harp and, to his accompaniment, Maria dances a graceful variation. Vatslav answers her with a dance full of speed and fire. The ball, which has calmed down, bursts forth again in a fiery mazurka.

The clatter of the horses of the Tartar horde is heard.

The chief of the castle guards, although mortally wounded, succeeds in warning the revellers of the surprise attack:

« *... multitudes of Tartars*
pour into Poland like a river;
Not with such terrible swiftness
does fire spread through the harvest. »

The men dash to find their swords and, returning, engage in a furious battle with the forces of Girei. Although the brave young men fight valiantly, they are soon overwhelmed by the overpowering numbers of the Tartars. The castle is set on fire. Vatslav and Maria, who is muffled in a scarf, try to escape. Vatslav fights bravely, killing many of the Tartars, but Girei himself arrives on the scene and blocks their path. Vatslav throws himself on the Khan and falls, killed by a stroke from a concealed dagger. Maria bows her head in the shawl and Girei, approaching her, casts off the shawl which covers her lovely features. Immediately he is struck by her beauty. In the light of the burning castle, Girei stands and admires the loveliness of Maria.

The Fountain of Bakhchisarai: Act II. A. Lapauri as Khan Girei.

Act II: Girei's harem in Bakhchisarai — the capital of the Crimean Tartars. The young wives of the Khan are playing and chatting in the morning sunlight. Eunuchs are watching the wives and the captive slaves mischievously tease the harem guards. The Georgian, Zarema, « the star of the harem », occupies first place among the wives.

Trumpets announce the return of Girei and his troops from their campaign in Poland. The women of the harem become excited in anticipation of seeing their master.

A curtain conceals the harem and warriors rush across the stage followed by Girei himself. Maria is carried to the harem on a litter perched on the shoulders of four of Girei's warriors.

Girei walks into the harem, takes off his armour, dons a golden robe and his crown and sits on his couch. Zarema greets him with dancing, exhibiting her beauty, but Girei is indifferent to her.

Maria, accompanied by an old servant, enters the harem carrying the harp which Vatslav played for her. She is an object of curiosity to the women of the harem with her fair hair and delicate features. But she walks slowly past the terrible Khan, aloof to his apparent admiration, absorbed in her grief for Vatslav. In vain his wives endeavour to divert the Khan with dances. He watches their movements apathetically. Zarema, who loves the Khan dearly, dances in an effort to regain his favour. But, thrusting Zarema aside, the Khan impetuously leaves his harem. The other wives ridicule the rejected Zarema. With malicious pleasure they gloat over her downfall, mimicing and mocking her. Girei reappears, lost in thought and Zarema embraces him but he shuns her affection and leaves without even a glance at her. Zarema faints.

Act III: Maria's bedchamber in the palace where Girei has quartered her with an old servant assigned to look after her. Maria sadly runs her fingers over the strings of Vatslav's harp, playing one of her native songs. Girei enters. He is experiencing a love never before known to him. Although he has loved many women, none had the power to arouse in him such strong, pure emotion as Maria. But Maria shows no signs of returning his affection. How can she love this mans, the cruel murderer of her Vatslav? Every attempt Girei makes to approach her only dismays and terrifies her. Realising that he cannot win her love by force, Girei humbly leaves the room.

Alone, Maria dreams of the past, of Vatslav, of their happy youth, their unclouded love. The old servant leads Maria to the couch

The Fountain of Bakhchisarai: Scene from Act I with N. Chorokova as Maria

and she falls into an uneasy sleep while the servant lies down on the floor by the doorway. Silently Zarema enters the room, clutching a dagger. She awakens Maria who gazes at her with fear and surprise. Zarema entreats Maria to « return » Girei to her. She tells Maria that she loves the Khan with a deep passion, that he is her life, her being.

In her surprise, Maria cannot answer and Zarema's pleas turn to threats: « I was born in the Caucasus and know how to handle a dagger. »

The old servant wakes up and, seeing Zarema, runs in terror for Girei. Girei, the servant and a harem guard dash into the room just as Zarema lifts the dagger to strike. Girei rushes towards her, trying to catch her but Zarema slips out of his grasp and stabs Maria in tre back.

In his fury and hopelessness, Girei is ready to kill Zarema but she herself goes to meet him, welcoming his dagger. Death at the hands of her beloved is not punishment but glory. Then Girei tells the guard to take Zarema away to await « a sentence worthy of her. »

Act IV: Girei sits morosely in his tower room surrounded by his Warriors. His troops, under the command of Nur Ali, return from another campaign. They bring with them enemy banners captured in battle and new captives for the harem. But Girei is indifferent both to the trophies and the new wives. Zarema is dragged into the room. She looks

The Fountain of Bakhchisarai: Scene from Act II with A. Lapauri as Khan Girei and L. Cherkassova as Zarema

The Fountain of Bakhchisarai: Scene from Act II with A. Lapauri as Khan Girei and R. Struchkova as Maria ▶

at Girei with a glance full of love but he turns his eyes away from her. She is led across to the tower battlements and, at a sign from Nur Ali, the executioners push Zarema over the steep precipice to the rocks below. The fiery dance of Nur Ali and his warriors does not soothe Girei. He dismisses his courtiers and warriors, making his way,

alone, to the « fountain of tears » which he has erected to the memory of the « sorrowful Maria. »

The soft murmur of the fountain brings to Girei the image of Maria. He reaches out his hands to her — but Maria is not there — only a shadow and a dream created by his imagination.

The Fountain of Bakhchisarai: Scene from Act II with Golovkina as Zarema

32

*The Fountain of Bakhchisarai: Scene from Act II
with M. Plisetskaya as Zarema*

The Fountain of Bakhchisarai: Scene from Act III with N. Chorokova as Maria, M. Plisetskaya as Zarema and K. Richter as Khan Girei

The Fountain of Bakhchisarai: Scene from Act III with P. Gussev as Khan Girei and G. Ulanova as Maria ▶

Fountain of Bakhchisarai: Scene from Act IV. The moment before Zarema is hurled to death from the battlements of Girei's palace

*Flames of Paris: Scene from Act II with E. Gikvaidze
as the actress Mirelle and A. Rudenko as the actor*

Flames of Paris

Ballet in 4 Acts and 5 Scenes

MUSIC: B. V. Asafiev

BOOK: N. D. Volkov and V. Dimitriev

CHOREOGRAPHY: V. Vainonen

First Moscow performance at Bolshoi Theatre 6-6-1933 with A. Abramova as Jeanne, A. N. Yermolaev as Philippe and M. Semyonova as Mirelle

It is 1792 and an armed detachement of Marseillais is on its way to Paris to join in the popular rising. In a village along their route, two Marseillais, Philippe and Jerome, make the acquaintance of the peasant, Gaspar and his children, Jeanne, Pierre and Jacques.

The Marseillais carry with them a revolutionary banner with the slogan: « Peace for the huts—War for the palaces. » The owner of the local castle, the Marquis of Beauregard, on his way back from hunting, notices the banner in Pierre's hands and orders his huntsmen to arrest the youth. The Marquis angrily throws the banner at Gaspar's feet and the old peasant picks it up. The huntsmen beat Gaspar and take him away to the castle.

The steward of the castle throws old Gaspar's poor belongings out of his hut. The Marseillais, Philippe and Jerome, call on the peasants to take part in the rising. An armed crowd gathers in answer to their call and storms the castle.

The Marquis de Beauregard manages to escape. The peasants join the Marseillais and, among the volunteers, are Jeanne and Pierre. The detachment sets off for Paris.

Act II: A Ball in the palace of Versailles. Artists of the court dance an intermezzo « The tricks of love. » The performance is interrupted by the appearance of the Marquis de Beauregard. He shows the assembled aristocrats the slogan of the revolutionaries and tells them about the peasants joining the revolt. There is alarm in the palace. The Marquis suggests to the courtiers that they should organise a counter revolutionary offensive and he writes a letter to the Prussians asking them for armed assistance. The King signs the letter. A banquet begins and the courtiers pass out of the salon. The actor, Antoine Mistral, finds the scroll containing the letter to the Prussians, which the Marquis has left behind. Returning to the salon, the Marquis sees the document in the actor's hands. Fearing that the latter may give away the secret, he kills Antoine.

The actress, Mirelle, finds the scroll in the dead man's hands, reads it and, overcome by her friend's death, decides to give the plot away to the Jacobins — the revolutionary party. In the distance is heard the strains of the Marseillaise — the song of the revolution. Mirelle flees from the palace.

Act III: A square in Paris where the revolutionaries have gathered, ready for a decisive conflict with the nobility. The Parisians welcome the detachment of Marseillais. Mirelle appears on the square and shows the revolutionaries the scroll with the text of the counter-revolutionary plot. The revolutionaries are filled with anger and indignation. The Jacobins lead into the square the Marquis whom they have taken under

arrest. The actress points to him as a leader of the plot. Seeing that his end is near, the Marquis tries to shoot the actress but Philippe skilfully manages to disarm him. The people's anger descends on the Marquis. They dance a Carmignole. With their arms in their hands, the revolutionaries set off to storm the royal palace of the Tuileries.

Flames of Paris: Scene from Act I. The Marseillais are joined by the villagers and leave for Paris

Flame of Paris: M. L. Gotlieb as Jeanne ▶

Act IV: A hall in the Tuileries. The aristocracy of the court is alarmed and dismayed. The sounds of revolutionary singing can be heard louder and louder from the street. An attempt by the officers of the palace to resist the revolutionaries fails. The people take possession of the palace.

Scene 2: A popular festival on a Paris square. The actress, Mirelle, dances for the people. Her performance is followed by popular dances. Jeanne and Philippe dance. The rejoicing ends in a general Carmagnole. The victorious and triumphant people carry shoulder-high the actress, Mirelle, who personifies the Goddess of Liberty.

Flames of Paris: Scene from Act III with Galina Ulanova as Mirelle

Flame of Paris: M. L. Gotlieb as Jeanne and V. Tsaplin as Gaspar

Flames of Paris: Act II. A ball at the Palace of Versailles

Flames of Paris: Act IV. A Paris Square. The people take the Palace

Flames of Paris: Scene from Act III. M. L. Gotlieb as Jeanne with members of revolutionary troups

Flames of Paris: Scene from Act I with G. Farma- nyantz as Philippe in foreground ▶

*The Sleeping Beauty: M. Plisetskaya as Aurora and
Y. Kondratov as Prince Desiré*

The Sleeping Beauty

Ballet in 3 Acts with a Prologue

MUSIC: P. I. Tchaikovsky

BOOK: M. Petipa after the fairy tale by Charles Perrault

CHOREOGRAPHY: M. Petipa

First Moscow performance at Bolshoi Theatre 17-1-1899 with L. Roslavleva as Aurora

Prologue: Outside the high walls of the royal castle, the herald's trumpets announce the birth of a daughter to the King — the Princess Aurora. Catalabut, the Master of Ceremonies, despatches messengers to all parts of the kingdom with invitations to the festival in honour of the Princess's christening. With great affection and reverence, all the good fairies are included in the invitation. Inside the King's palace, courtiers and guests anxiously await the nurses with the newly-born Princess. A heavy curtain rises and, at last, the processon enters the hall. The nurses tenderly place the princess in a cradle beside the throne and the guests come forward to present their gifts for the little Aurora. Trumpets announce the entrance of the King and Queen, who walk solemnly through the hall. The messengers who have been sent to the good fairies return to announce that all the invitations have been accepted and the fairies, followed by their suites, soon make their appearance with the Lilac Fairy leading them. All the fairies present the little Princess with gifts until only the Lilac Fairy is left.

But the christening ceremony is suddenly interrupted when Catalabut rushes in, horrified, to tell the King of the arrival of the Evil Fairy Karabos. Pushing the courtiers aside, terrified pages rush in confirming the dreadful news.

The lights fade and, in the ominous purple gloom, black warriors appear followed by Karabos, who drives into the castle on a chariot drawn by mice and rats and accompanied by her suite. She is very angry for Catalabut had naturally refrained from inviting such an evil guest to the christening. The courties vainly attempt to appease Karabos but she sweeps them aside with a flourish of her hand. Catalabut tries, in his turn, to pacify her but only provokes a further outburst of anger. Karabos throws herself on the unfortunate Catalabut and soon not a hair remains on the poor man's head. Then Karabos rushes to Aurora's cradle. None of the court even dare to breathe and the Queen begs Karabos for mercy but the Evil Fairy remains unmoved. She foretells a terrible fate for the Baby Aurora — on reaching the age of sixteen, she will prick her finger on a spindle and die. Then the Lilac Fairy steps forward. She has

Sleeping Beauty: V. Preobrazhenski as Prince Desiré

not yet given the baby Princess her own gift but it is beyond her power to dispel the dreadful curse of Karabos. She can, however, alter it by decreeing that, instead of dying, the Princess will fall into a deep sleep until a handsome Prince comes to waken her from the spell with his kiss.

Karabos, furious that her plans have been foiled, rushes from the palace. The good fairies bend over Aurora's cradle in farewell and disappear. The King summons his guards and commands that from that day on all spindles in his kingdom shall be destroyed.

Act I: The palace gardens on Aurora's sixteenth birthday. The guests have already assembled and Aurora's friends await her. In the meantime, they dance and make merry.

Catalabut meets the weavers who have come with birthday congratulations for the Princess. Their gift is a Gobelin tapestry with Aurora's portrait. The courtiers gather around the tapestry, admiring the weavers' skill.

Suddenly, Karabos, disguised as a lady of the court, emerges unnoticed from the crowd. Beckoning to a young weaver, she gives her a silver spindle and disappears. The weaver shows the spindle to her friends, thus attracting the attention of the courtiers. Catalabut is terrified at the sight of the spindle and snatches it away in panic, just as the King and Queen step out of the castle. The King is puzzled by the strange behaviour of his Master of Ceremonies. Catalabut, frightened out of his wits, is unable to utter a single word. He allows the spindle to slip out of his hand and fall at the King's feet.

The angry King asks Catalabut where he got the spindle and the Master of Ceremonies points to the weavers. The weavers, in their turn, point to the guests. The King summons the guard and orders Catalabut to find the guilty person immediately. The

Sleeping Beauty: R. Struchkova as Aurora

poor fellow takes up the search but no one can tell him who dared to violate the royal order. The King is beside himself with rage. Dreading the evil curse of Karabos, he commands his guards to arrest the weavers and Catalabut but they plead for mercy and the courtiers intervene on their behalf. The King hesitates but finally yields when the Queen adds her entreaties and forgives the weavers and Catalabut. The guards take the spindle away and young people begin a joyful dance.

Four princes arrive to ask the King for Aurora's hand. She appears amid the cheers of the guests and Catalabut introduces her

to the four suitors. They are deeply moved by her beauty and offer her their love. But Aurora cannot make up her mind and asks the Queen for her advice.

At that moment a mysterious lady gives Aurora a beautiful nosegay. Aurora distributes the flowers among the courtiers and finally only a silver spindle remains in her

Sleeping Beauty: Scene from Act I with L. Cherkasova in the centre as the Lilac Fairy

Sleeping Beauty: L. Cherkasova as the Lilac Fairy

hand, which had been hidden in the nose-gay. Her parents have abolished all the spindles in the Kingdom, so Aurora is intrigued by this strange object. Engrossed in the novelty, she does not notice the consternation and alarm of the court or heed the warnings being whispered at her from all sides. It is only a prick on the spindle that makes her raise her head. The courtiers rush up in alarm but an awful coldness has already laid its grip on her. She falls. The Queen, the King and Catalabut, the Princes

and all the courtiers bend over her in despair.

The mysterious lady watches the scene spitefully. Then she drops her cloak and the whole court recognises the Fairy Karabos. She gloats over her victory and vanishes with evil laughter.

The music of the Lilac Fairy stills the la-

Sleeping Beauty: Scene From Act I with R. Karelskaya as the Lilac Fairy

54

Sleeping Beauty: B. Khokhlov as Prince Desiré

Sleeping Beauty: L. Cherkasova as the Lilac Fairy

mentations of the guests as she tiptoes in with her wand. She assures the Court that Aurora is not dead—she has merely fallen into a trance and the day will come when the kiss of a handsome prince will rouse her from it. Accompanied by the King and Queen, the princes carefully carry the sleeping Aurora into the castle. Then the Lilac Fairy raises her magic wand and, as a final favour, she puts the entire court to sleep. The Lilac Fairy slowly walks among the sleepers, tenderly bidding them farewell. The trees and the grass begin to grow and the spellbound court slumbers on.

Act II: A century has passed and Prince Desiré and his friends enter a forest glade to rest after their hunting. Desiré is a bored young man who has been searching for perfection for so long that he has almost lost his illusions. Peasant maidens come in and a page asks them to gather flowers for the Prince and his suite. The courtiers begin a game of blind man's buff. They tie the Prince's eyes and the ladies each do their best to attract his attention. But their charms do not attract him. A peasant girl, returning to the glade, gives the Prince a bunch of lilacs and tells him the legend of the Sleeping Princess, far away in her enchanted castle. The Prince is greatly impressed by the legend and wanders off into the woods. The courtiers and the ladies are worried and go off in search of him. But Desiré has only been strolling among the trees, his mind full of the peasant girl's legend. He catches sight of the girl again and, as he comes towards her, her peasant dress falls away and the Prince sees the Lilac Fairy. He implores her to tell him more about Aurora and the Lilac Fairy waves her wand and shows him a vision of the sleeping beauty, guarded by the black suite of Karabos. Prince Desiré says he is ready to brave any danger to shatter the evil spell of Karabos and return Aurora to life—for she

Sleeping Beauty: M. Plisetskaya as Aurora and Y. Kondratov as Prince Desiré

is the image of perfection he has seen in his dreams.

The Lilac Fairy is now convinced that she has found one who can save the sleeping Princess. She takes him to the river where a boat awaits them and, together, they set out for the enchanted castle.

After a long voyage, Desiré and the Lilac Fairy arrive at the palace gates where the guards are still sleeping. The Prince must now go forward alone as only he can destroy Karabos' spell and wake Aurora. The windows, walls and doors of the castle are all

surrounded by an intricate mesh of webs netted with the baleful green of spiders' eyes, through which can be seen the flitting shapes of Karabos and her demons, who guard the castle so that no one can enter and awaken Aurora.

In a life-and-death struggle the Prince defeats the black suite of Karabos and the

Sleeping Beauty: Scene from Act I

Sleeping Beauty: M. Bogolyubskaya as Princess Florina and L. Zhdanov as Bluebird ▶

layers of the web break to reveal the couch of the sleeping beauty. A sheet of flames blazes up before him but the Prince courageously hurls himself into the fire and puts it out, destroying the last spell of Karabos. Desiré steps forward and wakens his princess with a kiss. The lights come on and, in the brilliant daylight, the court and Aurora wake up. The grateful King gives his consent to the marriage of the Prince and his daughter.

Act III: Aurora's wedding. The King, the Queen and the courtiers enter to the music of a polonaise, followed by Aurora and the Prince. Catalabut introduces all the guests from Fairyland who have come to the wedding. The merry festival begins.

Each of the fairies dance at Aurora's wed-

ding with the fairy-tale guests, including Puss in Boots, Little Red Riding Hood and the Grey Wolf, Tom Thumb and the Ogre, the Lilac Fairy and the fairies of Gems—Diamond, Gold and Silver—and lastly the Bluebird.

In a dazzling and brilliant spectacle, Aurora is married to her Prince.

Sleeping Beauty: Scene from Act II with R. Struchkova as Aurora and Y. Kondratov as the Prince

Sleeping Beauty: R. Struchkova as Aurora ▶

Sleeping Beauty: Scene from Act III with R. Struchkova as Aurora

*Sleeping Beauty: Scene from Act III with R. Struch-
kova as Aurora and Y. Kondratov as Prince Desiré*

Sleeping Beauty: Act III with M. Bogolyubskaya as Princess Florina and G. Farmanyantz as Bluebird

Sleeping Beauty: Scene from Act I with M. Plisetskaya as Aurora

Sleeping Beauty: with R. Struchkova as Aurora and A. Lapauri

Raimonda: Galina Ulanova as Raimonda

Sleeping Beauty: with R. Struchkova as Aurora and A. Lapauri

Raimonda: Galina Ulanova as Raimonda

Raimonda

Ballet in 3 Acts and 5 Scenes

MUSIC: A. K. Glazunov

BOOK: Lydia Pashkova and Marius Petipa

CHOREOGRAPHY: M. Petipa revised by A. Gorsky and I. Clustine

First Moscow performance at Bolshoi Theatre 23-1-1900 with A. Juri as Raimonda and V. I. Tikhomirov as Jean de Brien

The first act opens on the castle terrace of the noble family of Count de Doris, where the young friends of Raimonda, only child and heiress to the de Doris' wealth, are gaily dancing and making merry. Raimonda is renowned far beyond the borders of her native land for her beauty, charm and nobility of soul.

The blare of a trumpet interrupts the dancing and a friend of Raimonda's runs in to tell the dancers that the young Count de Brien, Raimonda's fiancé, is at the gate. The young people run away, watching the terrace from hiding places. Jean de Brien, followed by his warriors, walks onto the terrace. Finding nobody to receive him, he is embarrassed. However his desire to see his fiancé is so strong that he walks with determination up the steps leading to the castle.

The gateman, recognising Count de Brien, announces his arrival to Raimonda's mother, who comes out on the terrace to greet the young count, and Jean de Brien asks her permission to see Raimonda and bid her farewell before his departure for the crusades. Pages announce the arrival of Raimonda. Everybody leaves the terrace and only the two lovers remain. Jean gives Raimonda a bracelet as a pledge of his love and fidelity. The young people return and the noble young knight departs, taking with him the wishes of those who remain behind. Raimonda bows her head in sorrow as Jean disappears from sight. Suddenly a castle guard rushes on to the terrace to announce the arrival of an unknown man with an armed escort. The Countess, although she is worried by this unexpected guest, decides to receive the visitor. First one of the courtiers, Arslan, arrives to announce his master, the Emir Abdurakhman. The Emir is stunned by Raimonda's beauty of which he has heard so much. Raimonda feels a strange apprehension when she looks at the Emir. Abdurakhman presents Raimonda with rich gifts and tries to seduce her with a display of power and might. The sad Raimonda wants to call de Brien to her aid but, as she looks out to sea, she can make out only the dim silhouette of his ship fading into the distance. Thoughts of her loved one strengthen her courage.

Raimonda: Scene from Act I with M. Semyonova as Raimonda

As it grows dark, Raimonda goes indoors. The Countess, fulfilling her duty as a hostess, invites Abdurakhman to spend the night in the castle.

Scene 2: Raimonda's room. Raimonda plays her harp for her friends and dreams of her beloved. Some of the young people begin to dance and Raimonda, seeing her friends happy with each other, is even more sad. This scene is interrupted by the entrance of Nikosen, the page, who is followed by Arslan. Arslan, on the orders of Abdurakhman, brings trays of jewels for Raimonda. Upset by the Emir's persistent courting, Raimonda decides to send a letter to de Brien, asking him to return. Raimonda seals the letter with the bracelet which de Brien has given her and Nikosen, the page, volunteers to deliver the note to her fiancé.

Scene 3: On the steps of the terrace, Raimonda and her friends wish Nikosen a safe journey as he sets out to find de Brien. Her friends depart and Raimonda falls asleep on a bench overlooking the terrace. Her sleep is disturbed by nightmares. And then, still dreaming, she sees the same terrace decorated gaily and full of beautifully dressed, merry girls. A wonderful ship appears and de Brien with his warriors comes ashore. Raimonda is again with her beloved.

The fresh morning breeze awakens Raimonda and she leaves the terrace to return to her own room. On the steps of the castle she meets Abdurakhman, who has wandered about the castle grounds all night thinking of Raimonda. Abdurakhman tries to win her love · by force, but Raimonda rejects all his proposals. Abdurakhman, defeated, leaves the terrace in fury and Raimonda faints.

The day has now fully replaced the night shadows on the terrace and the castle is awake. Raimonda tells her friends what has happened during the night and her mother

is shocked at the behaviour of their guest. The offended Emir leaves the castle, still fuming. His look, directed at Raimonda, is full of malice.

Act II: The arrival of one of the Countess' relatives is being celebrated in the de Doris castle. Abdurakhman appears again—this time with a larger escort of armed warriors. He and his men block all the exits. The Emir emphasises his power by the servility he demands from the slave girls and bodyguards he has brought with him. However, Raimonda remains indifferent to him.

At a sign from Abdurakhman, the slaves begin a wild dance, during which they manage to separate Raimonda from her family and friends. Sensing danger, she tries to escape, but it is already too late. Arslan seizes her and runs towards the gate. He is on the point of rushing across the bridge when Jean de Brien bars his way. The forces of the Emir retreat before de Brien's courageous attack. Abdurakhman tries to strike Jean with his sword but the faithful Nikosen covers de Brien with his shield and he himself takes the death blow.

In the middle of the combat, Raimonda's father, Count de Doris, unexpectedly returns home. Upon hearing the events of the past few ways, Count de Doris decides that only a duel between Jean and Abdurakhman can decide the issue conclusively. The Emir attacks Jean with ferocious thrusts, but Raimonda's glance—full of love—gives courage to Jean and spurs him on until he strikes the fatal blow at Abdurakhman. The dying Emir is carried away by his courtiers and slaves.

De Brien is knighted by the Count de Doris, who joins his daughter's hands with de Brien's and gives them his blessing.

Act III: Guests have gathered. Heralds open the ball. Love and happiness have returned to the castle.

Raimonda: Scene from Act II with M. Semyonova as Raimonda and V. Golubin as Jean de Brien

*Bronze Horsemaon: Prologue. A. Radunski as Peter
the First about to launch a ship*

Raimonda: Scene from Act II with M. Semyonova as Raimonda and V. Golubin as Jean de Brien

*Bronze Horsemaon: Prologue. A. Radunski as Peter
the First about to launch a ship*

The Bronze Horseman

Ballet in 4 Acts and 6 Scenes with a Prologue of 3 Scenes

MUSIC: R. M. Glière

BOOK: P. Abolimov after the poem of Pushkin

CHOREOGRAPHY: R. Zakharov

First Moscow performance at Bolshoi Theatre 27-6-1949 with V. Preobrazhenski as Eugene, O. Lepeshinskaya as Parasha and M. Semyonova as Queen of the Ball

Prologue

« Alone beside the lonely sea
Enwrapt in lofty thoughts stood he;
Far reached his gaze: before him wide
The river flowed... »

In the semi-darkness can be seen the barren waters of the Neva, its soft swampy banks and the forests in the distance. Peter 1 appears in this wilderness.

« And thus he mused: ' From here, indeed
Shall we strike terror in the Swede;
And here a city by our labour
Founded, shall gall our haughty neighbour;
' Here cut' —so nature gives command—
' Your window through on Europe: stand
Firm-footed by the sea, unchanging.'
Ay, ships of every flag shall come
By waters they had never swum,
And we shall greet them heartily.' »

Scene 2 of the prologue: A wharf on the banks of the Neva. Out in the river is a Russian frigate from Peter's navy and, in the dockyard, is a huge ship being prepared for launching. Peter himself enters, surrounded by his shipbuilders.

A Dutch ship is being moored alongside.

Foreign sailors come down the gangway. Looking from one side to the other, they gaze with astonishment at the new Russia... ships of the Russian fleet, wharves, a city under construction, the Russian troops lined up on the shores.

The ceremony of the launching begins. Peter cuts the rope and the new ship slowly moves down into the Neva. A salute of guns is fired. The general gaiety is expressed in a Russian dance. Everybody dances... the shipbuilders, the carpenters, the masons and the sailmakers—the builders of the new Russian capital.

The Dutch sailors too take part in the dances which are full of Russian abandon and gaiety.

Scene 3 of the Prologue: Evening. Guests are assembling in Peter's summer palace. Dancing couples glide easily and smoothly over the polished floor. Peter enters with his suite. He chats in a lively and unaffected way with the shipbuilders and examines the model of a new gun, dreaming of new campaigns and voyages. Foreign envoys cluster

73

Bronze Horseman: A. Kuznetsov as Eugene

around. Europe is already beginning to pay court to Russia.

The « Queen of the Ball » opens the dancing and Peter dances the first dance with her. The dance changes into a game of Seek-your-partner. The one who is left without a lady is fined and must drink the cup of the great Eagle.

Late in the evening, the guests disperse and Peter remains behind. He bends over a plan of the city he is building. He imagines the wonderful panorama of the future St. Petersburg.

Act I:
« A century—and that city young,
Gem of the Northern world, amazing,
From gloomy wood and swamp upsprung,
Had risen, in pride and splendour blazing. »
It is the summer of 1824 and people are promenading on the Senate Square near the monument of Peter 1—the Bronze Horseman. This is the gay St. Petersburg of Pushkin's day. Here are officials, members of the forces, local citizens. Wandering artists perform. Sentries from the Moscow Lifeguards pass by with their band. This is the regiment which, in one and a half year's time, will rise under the banner of the Decembrists. Eugene enters. He has an appointment in the square with his sweetheart, Parasha. Eugene looks for Parasha in the crowd. But she is not here. Darkness comes on and the people gradually disperse. Eugene is alarmed.

Parasha enters and there is a joyous meeting between her and Eugene. But midnight is approaching. These are the last minutes of a tender farewell.

Act II: An autumn day on the island of Vassilevsky, where Parasha's house stands beside a spreading willow tree. Parasha's friends play games, sing songs and tell fortunes. Parasha's mother shows the girls how they used to dance in the olden days. Eugene appears at the gate and, hiding behind a tree, he watches the girls' games and admires his Parasha. Her friends, seeing Eugene, run away.

Left alone, Parasha and Eugene dream about the future. Eugene's dreams are modest. They are of Parasha and a quiet family life...

Heavy clouds gather in the sky and a storm blows up. Eugene must start for home before the bridges of the Neva are raised. He says goodbye to Parasha.

Bronze Horseman: Scene from Act I with E. Farmanyantz as Columbine and C. Chatilov as Harlequin

The wind gathers strength. Clouds roll fast across the sky. Parasha is anxious and begins to regret that she allowed Eugene to go away in such bad weather. She tries to call him back but it is too late.

Act III: The wind and the rain are beating against the window of Eugene's simple room,

and his thoughts are gloomy:
« *That from Parasha he must be*
Parted for some two days,, or three. »
The storm grows fiercer and the wind blows
like a tempest. The windows creak under
the heavy drops of rain and the sharp gusts
of wind. The dull sound of gunfire can be
heard in the distance. Eugene is worried.
Throwing on an overcoat, he rushes out of
the room.

Scene 2: The Senate Square is a scene of
great commotion. Crowds of sightseers have
gathered on the embankment.
« *Madder the weather grew, and ever*
Higher upswelled the roaring river
And bubbled like a kettle, and whirled
and like a maddened beast was hurled
Swift on the city. »
The people flee in terror and the square is
emptied. Eugene runs in. In front of him
is a vast gulf of water lashed by the wind.
The water rises higher and higher. Eugene
clims up on to a marble lion in front of a
building. Overturned sentry boxes, frag-
ments of fences and planks of wood float
past him. Sailors and fishermen rescue
drowning people.
« *Here, bare-headed,*
Pale, rigid, arms across his breast,
Upon the creature's marble crest
Sat poor Yevgeny. But he dreaded
Nought for himself. »
Eugene looks towards the island where he
left his Parasha. Full of yearning and an-
xiety, he abandons all discretion and, throwing himself into the water, he makes for a
boat, in the hope of crossing the torrential
waters of the Neva.

Act IV:
« *But now, with rack and ruin sated*
And weary of her insolence
And uproar, Neva, still elated
With her rebellious turbulence,
Stole back. »

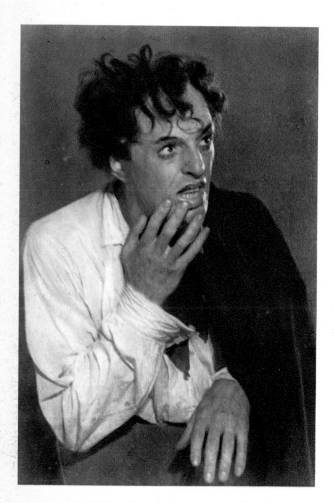

Bronze Horseman: V. Preobrazhenski as Eugene

Bronze Horseman: Scene from the Prologue. A. Radunski as Peter the First leads the dancers in the Palace with L. Cherkassova as the Queen of the Ball

Bronze Horseman: M. Bogolybskaya as Queen of the Ball

Eugene arrives in a canoe on the shore of the island of Vassilevsky.

« ... *Ah, what is here?*
Retreating, and again returning,
He looks—advances—looks again.
' Tis here they dwelt, the marks are plain;
There is the willow. Surely yonder
The gate was standing in the past;
Now, washed away. No house.' »

The despairing Eugene covers his face with his hands. His mind is full of distant memories. He cannot reconcile himself to Parasha's death. Her image haunts him. His sufferings make him lose his reason.

« *Alas, the tumult in his brain*
Had left him powerless to sustain
Those shocks of terror. »

Scene 2: The Senate square after the flood. The city has come to life again. Eugene roams along the embankment and urchins follow him, teasing him in his madness. The poor, mad Eugene stops by the monument to Peter 1 where, so recently, he used to meet Parasha. In front of him is the giant figure of the bronze horseman.

« *And now Yevgeny, with a shiver*
Of terror, felt his reason clear.
He knew the place, for it was here
The flood had gamboled, here the river
Had surged; here, rioting in their wrath,
The wicked waves had swept a path
And with their tumult had surrounded
Yevgeny, lions, square—and Him
Who, moveless and aloft and dim,
Our city by the sea had founded,
Whose will was Fate. »

The demented Eugene circles the monument. At that moment it seems to Eugene that Peter 1 is the cause of all his grief, with his plans to build a capital out of a bog and his artificial dykes and banks which had not stood up to the tidal waters. Then he imagines that the terrible Tsar has suddenly flared up in a fit of anger. Eugene rushes away in terror as if he hears behind him

Bronze Horseman: Galina Ulanova as Parasha

Bronze Horseman: Act II. Galina Ulanova as Parasha and M. Gabovich as Eugene

the thundering hooves of the bronze horseman.

He tries to run away but there is no escape.
The heavy heel of tyranny has trampled on
the life, the love and the dreams of a simple
man—one of many. Eugene and Parasha are
dead but the city of Peter's creation lives

Bronze Horseman: Scene from Act II with R. Struch-
kova as Parasha and A. Yermolaev as Eugene

and grows:
« *I love you, city of Peter's making;*
I love your harmonies austere,
And Neva's sovereign waters breaking
Along her banks of granite sheer. »
The orchestra plays a theme in praise of the
great city against a magnificent panorama
of St Petersburg.

Bronze Horseman: Galina Ulanova as Parasha and M. Gabovich as Eugene

Bronze Horseman: Scene with E. Farmanyantz as Columbine

Mirandolina: with Y. Kondratov as Fabrizio, O. Lepeshinskaya as Mirandolina and A. Radunsky as the Count

Mirandolina

Ballet in 3 Acts and 6 Scenes

MUSIC: Sergei Vasilenko

BOOK: P. F. Abolimov and V. A. Varkouitski from the play by Goldoni

CHOREOGRAPHY: V. Vainonen

First Moscow performance at Bolshoi Theatre 16-1-1949 with O. Lepeshinskaya as Mirandolina and Y. Kondratov as Fabrizio

Mirandolina is a ballet generally presented at the Bolshoi Filial. The play from which it was adapted is also given at one of the dramatic theatres and the Stanislavsky Theatre has presented a comic opera taken from the same play.

Act I: Early on a sunny morning in the courtyard of a hotel in Florence, belonging to the beautiful Mirandolina. In the middle of the courtyard, Fabriccio is busy cleaning shoes. But the work falls from his hands and he becomes absorbed in daydreams. For a long time now—and it seems to him, hopelessly—he has been in love with his beautiful mistress, Mirandolina.

Mirandolina enters. She pretends that she does not notice Fabriccio. But taking advantage of this favourable opportunity, he rushes towards her and declares his love for her.

Mirandolina herself is not indifferent towards her servant but, flirting with Fabriccio, she keeps him at a distance and will not disclose her secret. Finally, she becomes indignant at Fabriccio's persistence and sends him away. Distressed, Fabriccio leaves the courtyard. A crowd of street urchins rush in to inform Mirandolina of the arrival of a rich lodger. The Count Albaforita appears at the gates—rich and distinguished. All the servants of the hotel meet him. Seeing Mirandolina, the Count is immediately struck by her beauty. Escorted solemnly and gravely by the servants, the Count marches to the best room of the hotel which has been assigned to him.

The next guest enters the courtyard—the Marquis Forlipopoli, impoverished descendant of a once distinguished family, a little old man with a haughty bearing but empty pockets. He greets Mirandolina exquisitely, gallantly. But his compliments and polite salutations cannot take the place of money. Together with his servant, he is led to his room—the very worst in the hotel, under the staircase.

After a few minutes, the gates of the courtyard are again thrown open and a third guest enters—the cavalier Ripafratta. A passionate hunter, he is loaded down with hunting trophies. Ripafratta, in an excellent frame of mind from his success at hunting, orders his smart and saucy servant to take the game to the kitchen. The girls who serve in the hotel come running out at the sound of the noise, followed by Mirandolina. The cavalier becomes uneasy. A convinced woman-hater, he sees around him only women. In anger and exasperation, Ripafratta is ready to leave the hotel. But the ingenious and resourceful Mirandolina calls out her menservants. The cavalier is immediately soothed and decides to stay in the hotel after all. Mirandolina, giving him the key to his room, slyly holds out her hand for a kiss. With a scornful smile, Ripafratta turns away and runs hastily to his room.

Mirandolina is confused and does not understand the rude behaviour of the cavalier. She decides angrily to give this impudent aristocrat a good lesson and leaves the courtyard. Count Albaforita enters again, calling Fabriccio and asking him to arrange a rendezvous for him with Mirandolina. From under the stairs, the amorous Marquis Forlipopoli beckons to Fabriccio and hands him a letter for transmission to his mistress.

Recognising each other as rivals, the count and the marquis rush at each other furiously. Mirandolina returns and the count and the marquis, vying with each other, offer her the most exquisite compliments. Concealing her laughter, Mirandolina is equally amiable and flirtatious with both admirers.

Passions run high; the count quarrels with the marquis and challenges him to a duel. But the marquis has nothing with which to fight. His scabbard contains only a miserable, rusty fragment of a sword.

Albaforita mocks his unlucky opponent and, triumphant at his victory, he invites Mirandolina to dance with him. Fabriccio, standing in the background, is tormented with jealousy. Happy with his success, Albaforita presents Mirandolina with a pair of expensive earrings. Not wishing to take second place to the count, the Marquis Forlipopoli

*Mirandolina: O. Lepeshinskaya as Mirandolina and
Y. Kondratov as Fabrizio*

rushes to Mirandolina with his gift—an old, worn kerchief.

While amusing herself with these flirtations, Mirandolina accepts both gifts with equal courtesy, thus reconciling the rivals. Reassured, they leave.

Fabriccio is upset and expresses his jealousy to his mistress. Tossing aside his apron, he wants to leave the hotel and its artful innkeeper. With a sly smile, Mirandolina shows him a flower which she is keeping in memory of him. And the simple hearted Fabriccio is again full of hope and happiness.

Scene 2: Evening of the same day and the hotel courtyard is full of guests who have arrived for the carnival in Florence. Among the small tables roam street dancers, performing for the guests' amusement. Here one couple is dancing a fast and furious tarantella. Behind them, a gypsy girl is dancing with five young men. From the gates, groups of masqueraders and children in gaily coloured costumes run in. Merriment runs high and all dance masqueraders, guests and servants.

Count Albaforita comes out of the hotel, carrying bundles of cardboard boxes and packages. He offers splendid gifts to Mirandolina. But she is not interested in the gifts of the amorous Count. Happy and animated, she infects everyone with her own gaiety. Her tempestuous, solo dance rouses general delight.

Suddenly a crash is heard from above. Pillows and other household effects are being aimed from a window into the middle of the courtyard, straight at the dancers. The cavalier Ripafratta comes raging on to the staircase. He is indignant that his peace and comfort are being disturbed. All the merrymakers run away in confusion. Only Mirandolina is not frightened. With flirtatious kindness, she tries to subdue the cavalier's wrath. But he will not listen to her. Roughly pushing her away he rushes to his room.

Mirandolina, outraged and indignant, plans a suitable revenge.

Act II: The cavalier Ripafratta's room. He is amusing himself fencing with his servant. Supper is brought in but Ripafratta is not satisfied with any of the dishes. He is setting off for the kitchen to lodge a complaint with the cook, when, at the door, he collides with Mirandolina. She upbraids the servants and ousts them from the room.

Mirandolina herself begins to serve and entertain the cavalier. At first he treats her with his customary hostility. But Mirandolina is so obliging and attentive to all his caprices, her movements so polite and tender and the wine, which she serves, is so strong that, imperceptibly, he begins to take a fancy to his charming landlady. With skilful, graceful coquetry, Mirandolina compels the cavalier to declare his love for her. In a fit of passion, Ripafratta throws himself at Mirandolina's feet and she, in order to calm his fervour, pretends to faint. In confusion, Ripafratta calls the servants to his aid, catching up the 'fainting' Mirandolina in his arms. Startled and excited, Albaforita and Forlipopoli rush in followed by Fabriccio. They see the embarrassed Ripafratta with Mirandolina in his arms. She is at last 'recovering'.

Suddenly Mirandolina kisses Fabriccio and runs out. The count and the marquis make fun of the cavalier until he throws them out of his room.

Ripafratta is in despair. Ever stronger within his heart burns his love for Mirandolina. He drinks goblet after goblet of wine, and, looking at the portrait of Mirandolina in his room, he sinks into dreams of her. His dreams gradually pass into a deep sleep.

Scene 2: The sleeping Ripafratta dreams of Mirandolina. Girls rise up before him, reminding him of his love and enticing him to follow them. Suddenly the dream fades and Ripafratta wakes up on the floor. Coming to his senses, he kneels before Mirandolina's portrait. His servant, who has just come in, sneers at his master, the woman-hater has become the prisoner of a woman.

Scene 3: A moonlit night. In the garden under Mirandolina's window, Fabriccio is singing a serenade. She comes out on to her balcony and Fabriccio rushes towards her with confessions of love. But a noise is heard and the count enters the garden too, hoping to sing his serenade under Mirandolina's window. In order to confuse the count, Fabriccio hangs Mirandolina's coloured shawl on Ripafratta's balcony. Then he and Mirandolina hide themselves in the shadows. Secretly and stealthily, his head covered by a cape, Count Albaforita creeps into the garden, followed by the musicians he has hired. He notices the balcony with Mirandolina's shawl, gives the musicians some money and they begin to play.

From the other side of the courtyard the marquis enters. Behind him his servant is dragging an enormous ladder and a basket of roses. The marquis is already preparing to climb the ladder to the balcony but the count rushes across and stops his rival. A scuffle takes place. At this moment the cavalier Ripafratta, suddenly awakened, springs from his balcony and, in a frenzy, with his sword in his hand, throws himself on the count. Struggling, the count retreats and Ripafratta pursues him. Mirandolina and Fabriccio reappear in the now deserted garden. At last they are alone and Fabriccio has a chance of talking with her. Mirandolina no longer hides her feelings for Fabriccio.

Act III: The city square at night with the carnival in full swing. With noise and merriment, the young people, in masks and gaily coloured costumes, dance to the accompaniment of guitars and tambourines. One dance is rapidly followed by another. A Spanish dance and the traditional dance of « The Devil » follow the fantastic and amusing dance of the clowns. The throng of dancers increases and the whole square revolves in a whirlwind tarantella.

Pushing people aside, the confused Marquis Forlipopoli runs in. After him the count Albaforita and the cavalier Ripafratta burst through the crowd still fighting with each other. They knock people down, brandish their swords and continue their duel in the middle of the square. Mirandolina arrives and stops their duel with one gesture. Her admirers again hope for the favour of the charming beauty. But, at a signal from Mirandolina, Fabriccio returns their gifts to the count and the marquis. They are stunned but Ripafratta is triumphant, believing he is the lucky one. He is full of happiness and joy, but Mirandolina introduces Fabriccio to everyone as her fiancé. In despair, Ripafratta runs from the square with the count and the marquis fleeing behind him. Laughing and ridiculing them, the crowd pursues the three thwarted suitors.

The square empties and Mirandolina and Fabriccio perform, at last, their dance of love.

The people, having driven away the aristocrats, return to the square and congratulate the bride and bridegroom. As a sign of their indissoluble union, Mirandolina ceremoniously hands over to Fabriccio the keys to her hotel.

*Fadetta: Act III with A. Lapauri as Andre and
I. Tikhomirnova as Madelon*

Fadetta

Ballet in 3 Acts and 4 Scenes

MUSIC: L. Delibes

BOOK: L. M. Lavrovsky and V. Soloviev after the poem of Georges Sand

CHOREOGRAPHY: L. M. Lavrovsky

First Moscow performance at Bolshoi Theatre 20-6-1952 with O. Lepeshinskaya as Fadetta

A tumbledown cottage near a stream in the middle of a wood, where Grandmother Ursula lives with her grandchildren, Fadetta and Sylvester.

Fadetta runs out of the wood, throws down the armful of firewood she has collected, picks up a bucket and goes to fill it at the stream. Sylvester runs after his sister and starts to play a game of horses with her. But when their grandmother comes out of of the cottage and begins to hang out the medicinal herbs she has picked for drying, Fadetta stops playing with her brother and runs to help the old woman. She knows that her grandmother is old and ill and that her brother is still very young and sometimes wonders what will happen to them.

Suddenly the old woman is alarmed by the sound of hunting horns and tries to hurry her grandchildren inside the cottage. Ursula and her grandchildren are poor and, when the young men of the village are on their way back from hunting, they often insult the old woman if they happen to meet her.

But Sylvester is interested to see the hunters and climbs into his favourite hiding place in an old tree to watch, while Fadetta decides to hide somewhere close by and keep an eye on her brother.

The hunters carry in a wild boar which they have killed and the village girls, led by Madeleine, the daughter of Barbo, the richest man in the village, run in to meet them. One of the hunters, Rene, boasts that the success of the day's hunting was due to himself. But the girls, laughing, do not believe him, saying that it was probably Andre, the best hunter in the village, who killed the boar. Rene, feeling insulted, walks away towards the tree. But, hearing a rustling up above, he decides that there must be some animal hiding there and, with his gun in his hand, he creeps forward, intending to prove his mettle as a hunter in front of them all. But it is only Sylvester who appears out of hiding place.

Rene is piqued and wants to vent his anger on the boy. But Fadetta runs out of the house to shield her brother. Madeleine and her friends begin to joke about Fadetta and mock her—the ragged clothes she is wearing

Fadetta: O. Lepeshinskaya as Fadetta and V. Preo-brazhenski as Andre

and her unkempt hair. Andre and his friend, Jean, stop them.

Madeleine, although she likes Andre, is annoyed with him for interrupting their game. « Why come to the defence of these nobodies? » she demands and, together with Rene and her friends, she laughs at Andre.

But, knowing Andre's strength and realising that he always means what he says, the other hunters check Rene, who is becoming foolhardy, and they start a dance to make everyone forget the incident.

Madeleine dances with Rene, hoping to make Andre jealous. Nettled because she has not attracted his attention, Madeleine then runs towards Ursula's house and tears down the herbs which Ursula and Fadetta had hung up so carefully. This at lasts rouses Andre and he drives her and her friends away from the cottage. His behaviour has now infuriated Madeleine and she angrily tramples on the flowers in front of the cottage.

Coming out of her house, Ursula picks up her scattered herbs and Andre bends down to help her, thus increasing Madeleine's indignation. Wanting to please Madeleine, Rene fires his gun to startle Ursula but Andre snatches the gun from his hands and the affronted Rene backs away. Upset because the insolent Madeleine and her friends have scattered the herbs in all directions and trampled on her new plants, Fadetta runs up to Madeleine and begins to scold her but the hunters come to Madeleine's assistance and attack Fadetta. Only Andre springs to the girl's defence. Rene throws a stone at Fadetta and she falls but soon gets up again and laughs gaily as if nothing had happened.

Andre, having warned the hunters to leave her alone, goes off into the woods by himself and the village girls abandon their tormenting.

The clearing is deserted and Fadetta, making certain that everybody has gone away, comes out from behind a tree clump. Andre, coming out of the wood again, sees the weeping girl and, going up to her, tries to comfort her gently. It is the first time that Fadetta has ever heard warm and sympathetic words from a strange man.

But Andre also rebukes Fadetta. Why does she tease the village girls? Why does she behave like a boy? Why does she go around looking so bedraggled and dressing like an urchin? Fadetta is confused when she hears this criticism. She had not realised that

Fadetta: Act III with K. Richter as Jean, T. Bessmert-nova as Jeanette and H. Orlovskaya as Celestine

there were faults on both sides she promises. Andre that she will try and mend her ways in future. Andre bids her a friendly farewell and goes away. But Fadetta stands for a long time staring after him. She cannot analyse her feelings. Something new fills her soul.

Act II: In Barbo's house, they are hoping

93

to celebrate the engagement of Madeleine and Andre. For many years this has been the fondest wish of Barbo and his friend Prosper, Andre's father. Barbo sits by the open window, suffering from the heat. Madeleine is posing for an artist who is painting her portrait. But she is bored with the artist and sitting still for so long and suddenly decides to create a diversion, making such a noise and din that poor Barbo plugs his ears with his fingers and rushes off into another room and the artist stops working. Peeping round the door, Madeleine's friends

enter the room. They part and Rene comes out from behind them.

Barbo comes back unexpectedly. Seeing Rene in his house on the day of Madeleine's betrothal, he is beside himself with anger, and drives the young people out of the room. The matchmaking mothers of the village come in with their eligible sons. Prosper

Fadetta: E. Gikvaidze as Fadetta and A. Lapauri as Andre

Fadetta: Act III with E. Gikvaidze as Fadetta and A. Lapauri as Andre

*Fadetta: Scene from Act III with M. Lepeshinskaya
as Fadetta and A. Lapauri as Andre*

also arrives and Madeleine complains to him about Andre's behaviour yesterday and about Fadetta's impudence. At last Andre himself appears reluctantly.

At this moment, Fadetta runs past the window, pursued by the village boys. Somebody throws a stone which hits her and everybody in the room laughs spitefully. But Andre is exasperated. Learning of his father's wish that he should announce his betrothal to Madeleine, he protests and refuses his father's blessing.

Andre tries to hurry away but Barbo locks the door, stuffing the key in his pocket. Then in order to cover up the unpleasantness, Barbo proposes a toast for Andre and Madeleine. Soon everybody slips quietly away, leaving the young couple alone. Andre has gone over to the window and Madeleine tries to attract his attention. But Andre is merely annoyed by her advances and pushes her away. The matchmaking mothers and their sons, hearing the quarrel, come back into the room and try to reconcile Madeleine and Andre. A servant begins to hand round food and wine and the room becomes gayer. Only Andre refuses to enter into the party spirit and, at the first opportunity, he snatches the key from Barbo, unlocks the door and runs off.

Barbo stands there astonished as Prosper goes off after his son and Madeleine, seated at the table, tries to persuade her other elegible young suitors to avenge themeselves on Andre.

Scene 2: A small clearing on the edge of the wood with the ruins of an old fortress in the distance, which is Fadetta's favourite place for solitude. Sitting on a pile of stones, while Sylvester plays near her, she recalls the details of her meeting with Andre.

The sound of footsteps makes them hide behind a stone as Rene and Madeleine enter, looking for a solitary place for a rendezvous. But Madeleine does not like the ruins and they go off.

Depressed by the scene in Madeleine's house, Andre roams through the woods with his gun. Passing the old fortress, he hears Sylvester's voice, comes out into the clearing and sees Fadetta.

At the sight of Andre, Fadetta does not know what to do. Taken unawares, she tries to tidy her unkempt hair in confusion and Sylvester quickly hides behind a large stone. Deciding that he is not a very welcome guest, Andre turns to leave but Fadetta catches him up, takes the gun from his shoulder and leads him back.

Andre is overwhelmed by a new feeling on this second meeting with Fadetta. She is so sincerely glad to see him and neither of them can hide their emotion, holding hands with deep love. Suddenly from among the ruins of the fortress, Rene's head appears from behind a stone. He sees Fadetta and Andre and hurries quickly away.

As darkness falls, Fadetta runs up to her brother and sees that he is already asleep. Andre gently wakens the boy and offers to carry him home. The three of them are happily departing when Rene and Madeleine come towards them. Rene is in love with Madeleine and wants to convince her that Andre does not give her a second thought. Madeleine steps forward and, laughing spitefully, runs away, with Rene at her heels.

Andre frowns after them while Fadetta weeps bitterly nearby and Sylvester tries to calm her.

Act III: It is a sunny day and there is a holiday in the village. Festive tables are set out in the square in front of the inn while a cook, the innkeeper's wife and servants are scurrying around. Noticing some paupers sitting at one of the tables, the cook chases them away on the orders of the organiser of the holiday. The peasants retreat gloomily behind the inn fence and, having assured himself that everything is ready for the guests, the organiser of the holiday opens the celebrations. All the rich people of the village have assembled—only Andre is absent.

The festivities commence with an old village custom—the ceremony of the distribution of the ribbons. All the men present their ribbons to the ladies of their choice. Taking advantage of Andre's absence, Rene attaches his ribbon to Madeleine's blouse. But soon after, Andre comes into the square with his friend Jean. Without replying to his father's scolding for being late and for wearing his ordinary clothes, Andre takes his ribbon and sits at a table.

The dancing begins. Andre, noticing Sylvester standing on the road, calls the boy to him and gives him his ribbon to take to Fadetta.

Prosper and Barbo demand that Andre should dance with Madeleine and Andre agrees but, seing that Rene and Madeleine are exchanging glances over his shoulder all the time, Andre makes this an excuse to stop dancing and Rene and Madeleine finish the dance together. The feast becomes rowdier and more drunken as one dance follows another. Already Prosper, Barbo and both of the matchmakers have done a dance when suddenly Fadetta appears in the square with Andre's ribbon on her dress.

The dancing and the gaiety cease abruptly. Turning their backs on Fadetta, the villagers return to their tables and sit down. But Fadetta does not notice this unfriendly reception. She has eyes for no one but Andre as she wonders if he will notice the change in her appearance for she has carried out his wish—her hair is brushed and she no longer looks like an urchin boy.

Andre, greeting her with delight, also ignores the villagers and dances with Fadetta. The daughters of the rich men of the village are insulted that Fadetta is wearing one of their ribbons. Tearing off their own ribbons in disgust, they throw them on the ground. But apparently unaware of his surroundings,

Andre continues to dance with Fadetta and, at the end of the dance, as village custom demands, he bends forward and kisses her. This fans the villagers' anger into flames. Prosper snatches Fadetta's ribbon and orders her to leave the square immediately. But Andre restores the ribbon to her and deliberately kisses her a second time. The rich men of the village give way to such fury that at last Andre sees that he has nothing in common with his father and his father's friends and will have to build his future away from them.

Prosper feels that Fadetta is the cause of all the trouble and, wanting to punish her, he

Fadetta: Scene from Act III

rushes towards her and is about to strike her when Andre catches him by the arm and throws him to the ground. The paupers, who have been watching the whole scene from behind the inn fence, now rush into the square and come to Andre's defence. Andre goes up to Fadetta and, taking her in his arms, leaves the village with her forever.

Swan Lake: Galina Ulanova as Odette

Swan Lake

Ballet in 4 Acts

MUSIC: P. I. Tchaikovsky

BOOK: V. P. Begitchev and Geltser

CHOREOGRAPHY: M. Petipa and Leo Ivanov revised by A. Vaganova

First Moscow performance at Bolshoi Theatre 20-2-1877 with I. Karpakova as Odette-Odile

A brilliant autumn afternoon in the garden of the castle of the reigning princess. The young Prince Siegfried, her son, and his friends are making the forest glade echo with their merriment, as they celebrate his coming of age. The amusing dances of the clown are followed by the graceful dances of the girls and their cavaliers. The gaiety is interrupted for a moment with the entry of the Princess, who informs her son that tomorrow at the Palace Ball he will have to choose his bride from a number of girls who have been invited to the celebration. His mother's wish depresses Siegfried who has not yet met the girl of his dreams. After the Princess leaves, the young people resume their dancing—even Siegfried's old tutor taking part in the dance.

Twilight comes and the young people disperse. Siegfried is melancholy. He does not wish to part with his life of freedom in this happy circle of friends. At the same time, the image of a girl whom he might love appears to him. But where is she? Where will he find such a girl?

The sight of a flock of swans, flying over-head, rouses Siegfried from his reverie and, arming themselves with cross-bows, he and his friends set forth on the hunt.

Act II: In the midst of a forest thicket is a deep lake. On its shore rises the gloomy ruins of an ancient castle. At midnight, when all the surrounding nature sinks into a deep sleep, a procession of white swans swims along the lake. Arriving on the shore, the swans circle in a slow, bird-like, dance. Siegfried, whose attention is attracted to a beautiful swan illuminated by the shimmering light of the moon, appears. Taking aim, Siegfried is about to let loose his arrow, when he stops, surprised by the sudden transformation of the Swan into a beautiful Princess—the Princess Odette. The girl swans encircle Siegfried and Odette tells him of the secret spell which has been cast on her and her friends. An evil genius has transformed them from maidens into swans and, only at night, beside these ruins, can they again take on their human form. Touched by Odette's sorrowful tale, Siegfried proposes to kill the Evil Genius. But Odette answers

Swan Lake: I. Tikhomirnova as Odette

sadly that this will not save them from the sorcery. Only the supreme love of one who has never yet sworn his love to anyone will lift the spell.

The Evil Genius, who dwells in the ruins of the castle, overhears the conversation between Odette and Siegfried. He will not let Odette out of his power.

Siegfried is filled with love and pity for the beautiful Odette. He swears his love and faithfulness to her and invites her to tomorrow's ball where he is expected to name his bride. But Odette cannot appear before human people while still under the evil spell. She warns Siegfried that the Evil Genius, with the aid of his craft and cunning, will try to compel him to break his oath of faithfulness and, if the oath is broken, then she and her friends will perish.

Dawn comes. The girls must again turn into swans. Siegfried is confident of his feelings —he will free Odette from the power of the Evil Genius.

Act III: The hall in the castle of the Princess. Guests who have been invited to the Ball are being announced with fanfares. Among the guests are six girls from among whom the Princess wishes Siegfried to choose a bride. But the Prince is indifferent to these princesses—he is full of memories of the beautiful swan-maiden, Odette.

The Evil Genius, in the robes of a knight of the Black Swan, enters the ballroom accompanied by his daughter, Odile, who bears a striking resemblance to Odette. Siegfried is bewitched and decides that this is his chosen bride—Odette.

The ball begins, the clown buffooning and the foreign guests dancing in the style of their native countries. Spanish, Neapolitan, Hungarian and Polish dances interchange. Odile dances last. The Evil Genius orders her to captivate Siegfried and provoke from him a declaration of love—compelling him to break his word to Odette and leave her

Swan Lake: M. Plisetskaya as Odette

still under the power of his sorcery. Siegfried is entranced by Odile and dances with
her, disregarding the swan which flies past
the window of the castle.

Siegfried announces to his mother that he
has decided to marry the daughter of the
Knight of the Black Swan. The Evil Genius
is exultant.

The oath is broken and now Odette and
her friends will perish.

With a mocking laugh, Odile and the Evil
Genius point to the image of Odette which
appears in the castle window, as Odile and
her father rush from the castle. Siegfried,

realising that he has been deceived, hurries
to the lake in despair.

Swan Lake: Galina Ulanova as Odette

Act IV: The shore of the lake. Overcome by
her grief, Odette tells her friends of Siegfried's treachery. The swan-maidens are sad
—their hope of freedom is lost. But Siegfried runs in. He has not forgotten his oath

Swan Lake: M. Bogolyubskaya as Odette

and has not ceased to love Odette. There, in the castle, he saw only his Odette in the image of Odile and it was to her that his pledge referred. The Evil Genius, in his fury, calls the elements to battle against the lovers.

A storm begins, lightning flashes, thunder rumbles and the wind tears at the branches of the trees. But nothing can kill the bond

of love between Odette and Siegfried. Feeling that his power is lost, the Evil Genius demolishes his castle, trying to block the way of the lovers. He engages in single combat with the Prince and is killed. Love has conquered and Odette and Siegfried, surrounded by the happy swan-maidens, meet the first rays of the rising sun.

Swan Lake: Act II with M. Plisetskaya as Odette and V. Preobrazhenski as Prince Siegfried

Swan Lake: Act I. A. Yermolaev as Prince Siegfried

Swan Lake: M. Plisetskaya as Odette

Swan Lake: R. Struchkova as Odette and V. Preo-brazhenski as Prince Siegfried

Swan Lake: Two scenes from Act II

Swan Lake: R. Struchkova as Odette ▶

*Swan Lake: Scene from Act II with M. Plisetskaya
as Odette and Y. Kondratov as Prince Siegfried*

*Swan Lake: R. Struchkova as Odette and V. Preobra-
zhenski as the Prince*

Swan Lake: O. Lepeshinskaya as Odile and V. Preo-brazhenski as Prince Siegfried

*Swan Lake: Act III with M. Pliseiskaya as Odile
and V. Golubin as Prince Siegfried*

*Swan Lake: O. Lepenshinskaya as Odile and V. Preo-
branhenski as Prince Siegfried*

*Swan Lake: Act III with M. Plisetskaya as Odile
and V. Preobrazhensky as Prince Siegfried*

*Swan Lake: Act III with M. Plisetskaya as Odile
and V. Golubin as Prince Siegfried* ▶

Romeo and Juliet: Act. III Scene I with Galina Ula-
nova as Juliet and M. Gabovich as Romeo

Romeo & Juliet

Ballet in 3 Acts and 13 Scenes with Prologue and Epilogue

MUSIC: S. Prokofiev

BOOK: L. M. Lavrovsky and S. F. Prokofiev after Shakespeare

CHOREOGRAPHY: L. M. Lavrovsky

First Moscow performance at Bolshoi Theatre 28-12-1946 with Ulanova as Juliet, M. Gabovich as Romeo, A. Yermolaev as Tybalt and S. Koren as Mercutio

Romeo, Friar Laurence and Juliet appear in a triptych. The light goes out. The triptych disappears and the spectator sees a *piazza* of the town of Verona in Italy.

Act I: Early on a misty morning. Romeo cannot sleep and roams through the streets of Verona.

As soon as the first early risers appear, Romeo hides in the nearest side street. A flower-seller runs across the bridge on her way to the river to buy fruit, delivered to the city in boats. Young people walk past. A priest goes to the morning service. The Capulet servants, Gregorio, Samson and Petro, shivering in the morning cold, come out of their master's house.

The waitresses in the café, with sleepy faces, lazily set out tables and chairs on the sidewalk. Gregorio, Samson and Petro go up to them as to old acquaintance. They exchange jokes and dance. Montague's servants, Abramio and Balthazzar, come out into the *piazza*. The Capulet servants are longing to fight with them. Capering around on different sides so as not to let Montague's servants leave the *piazza*, they start teasing them and then begin a fight. When one of Montague's servants is wounded, Montague's nephew, Benvolio, comes running up and, drawing his sword, orders the Capulet servants to withdraw. Capulet's nephew, Tybalt, appears, insults Benvolio and challenges him to a duel.

The fight between the supporters of the Montagues and the Capulets reopens. At the height of the fray, Paris appears. He has come to ask for the hand of Capulet's daughter, Juliet. But Capulet, running out of his house with his sword in his hand is eager to take part in the encounter. Montague hurries towards him and the fight becomes more heated. The town is awakened by the loud noises of the alarm. Citizens rush in from all sides and the Duke of Verona comes onto the *piazza* with his guard. The people ask him to defend them. The Duke orders swords and rapiers to be put away. One of the members of the guard displays the Duke's proclamation that whoever dares to draw swords in the streets of Verona will be punished by death.

Everybody disperses. Tybalt and his friends
go out waving their swords threateningly at
the Montague supporters.

Scene 2: Juliet's room in Capulet's house.
Juliet plays mischievously with her nurse.
But her gaiety suddenly leaves her when she
sees her mother entering. Her mother stern-
ly tells Juliet that Paris is asking for her
hand. Juliet is astonished. She is so young.
But her mother takes her to the mirror and
shows her that she is now a woman. Juliet
is confused.

Scene 3: Front stage: The Capulet servants
carry loaded platters—meat, fruit and pas-
tries, past the major-domo on their way
to the feast. The front curtain rises and
richly clad guests pass in ceremonious pa-
rade on their way to a feast in Capulet's
house.

Juliet's girl friends, accompanied by trouba-

*Romeo and Juliet: Act I Scene 2 with Galina Ula-
nova as Juliet and L. Olenina as her Nurse*

Romeo and Juliet: Act I Scene 3 G. Ulanova as Juliet and E. Timoshenkaya as her mother.

dours, flit by followed by Paris with his page. Front Stage: Mercutio and Benvolio appear. They hear the sound of music and decide to gate-crash the ball. They persuade Romeo to go into the palace with them and the three of them gaily don masks.

Scene 4: The Ball at the Capulets. The guests are seated at the tables with quiet dignity. Juliet and Paris are surrounded by a group of friends. Troubadours entertain the young girls and dances begin. After the stiff and formal cushion dance of the elderly

couples, Juliet's dance seems like the fluttering of a breeze. All the guests are delighted. During Juliet's dance, Romeo and his friends enter the room. Romeo is carried away by Juliet's beauty. He cannot take his eyes off her.

The solemn atmosphere of the ball is broken by Mercutio's tomfoolery. Romeo goes up

Romeo and Juliet: Act II Scene 1. The Piazza in Verona. E. Kashani as the Jester

*Romeo and Juliet: Act I Scene 4 with E. Gikvaidze
as Juliet and Y. Hofman as Romeo*

to Juliet and declares his passion for her in a madrigal. Juliet suddenly pulls the mask from his face and is struck by his handsome features. This is a man, with whom she could fall in love. Tybalt interrupts them, recognises Romeo as an enemy of the Capulets and hurries to Capulet to tell him of Romeo's impudence. The ball continues. Juliet's friends and the troubadours dance. Front stage: The guests disperse. The nurse tells Juliet that the young man who has captured her heart is the son of Montague, Capulet's enemy.

Scene 5: A garden by moonlight. Juliet looks serenely into the misty distance, dreaming of Romeo. Her lips frame loving words. Her face is lit with a smile. Romeo enters the garden and stretches out a hand to her in passion and entreaty.

Romeo and Juliet: Act II Scene 3 with S. Koren as Mercutio and Y. Sangovich as the Servant Girl

Act II: Noise and gaiety on a *piazza* in Ve-

126

rona. Citizens in festive dress come in from all sides. The owner of the cafe serves his patrons. Benvolio and Mercutio joke with the girls. The young people dance, beggars hang around, old people squat phlegmatically—fishermen and fruitsellers.

A gay carnival procession passes by. They all dance around the image of the Madonna.

The nurse, accompanied by Petro, is seeking Romeo in order to give him a letter from Juliet.

Mercutio and Benvolio are teasing her when

Romeo and Juliet: Act II Scene 1 with I. Olenina as the Nurse and A. Varlamov as Benvolio

Romeo appears and, after a little sideplay, the nurse gives him the letter. Romeo reads Juliet's letter with joy. She has agreed to become his wife.

Scene 2: Friar Laurence passes his day in tranquil solitude. He take a flower and looks at it. In the flower, which seems so

Romeo and Juliet: with Galina Ulanova as Juliet,
M. Gabovich as Romeo and A. Bulgakov as Friar
Laurence

beautiful and fragile, a fatal poison has been poured. Its scent it pleasing but whoever breathes it in must die. And, just as joy and death are hidden in this flower, so in the hearts of men good and evil live side by side.

Romeo appears. He begs Friar Laurence to marry him to Juliet. Laurence is moved and embraces Romeo, promising his help, hoping by this marriage to reconcile the opposing houses of the Montagues and the Capulets. The delighted Romeo gathers flowers for Juliet from Laurence's desk. Among the flowers he finds a skull, picks it

Romeo and Juliet: Act. II with Galina Ulanova as Juliet, M. Gabovich as Romeo and A. Bulgakov as Friar Laurence

up and reflects. The flowers fall, one by one, from his hands. Friar Laurence comforts Romeo. Juliet appears, Romeo gives her his hand and Laurence carries out the wedding ceremony.

Front stage: A gay procession. Mercutio and Benvolio, surrounded by young girls, come at the end of the procession. Mercutio buys a whole basket of flowers from the flower-seller and generously distributes oranges to his lady friends.

Scene 3: The same *piazza* full of merry citizens. Mercutio and Benvolio have taken their places in the cafe with their friends. Young people dance around them. Tybalt appears on the bridge and, seeing his enemies from the house of Montague, hurries down. Drawing his sword, he attacks Mercutio. Romeo, entering the *piazza,* tries to make peace between them. But Tybalt insults Romeo and Mercutio will not listen to him. The duel between Tybalt and Mercutio is resumed. Romeo again tries to separate them but Tybalt, seizing a suitable moment during the pause, treacherously lunges at Mer-

cutio, who dies gallantly, with a jest still on his lips. Mercutio's death angers Romeo. He challenges Tybalt to a duel and the heated fight ends in Romeo's victory. Tybalt is killed. The frightened Benvolio leads Romeo away from the *piazza.* The relations of the dead Tybalt swear eternal vengeance, over his body, on the house of Montague.

Romeo and Juliet: Act. III Scene 3 with E. Gikvaidze as Juliet

Romeo and Juliet: Act. III Scene 3 with Galina Ulanova as Juliet ▶

Romeo and Juliet: Act III Scene I with Galina Ulanova as Juliet and M. Gabovich as Romeo

Act III: The thin light of dawn slants through the windows of Juliet's room. Romeo kneels at the feet of his beloved wife. Juliet looks lovingly at his face as if trying to remember his features forever. Jumping up, Romeo opens the window wide and the sun's rays burst into the room. It is time for the lovers to part. People have already woken up in the house and there can be no further delay. Juliet tries to keep him with her just a little longer but finally agrees to a brave farewell. Romeo throws on his cloak, embraces Juliet and goes out through the window. Juliet's nurse comes into the room with her parents and Paris behind her. Juliet's mother tells her that her marriage with Paris has now been arranged. But Juliet greets Paris coldly and he leaves the room sadly, feeling that he will never win her love. Juliet's parents shower her with scoldings and reproaches. Her father threatens to drive her out of the house. Juliet is in despair. But then she remembers Friar Laurence and decides to seek his advice.

Scene 2: Juliet, breaking in on Friar Laurence's solitude, falls on her knees before him and begs his help. Taking a knife, she is ready to kill herself. Laurence takes the knife from Juliet and, pitying her in her grief, gives her a sleeping draught. He whispers to Juliet that the only way in which she can avoid her marriage to Paris is to drink this potion. After taking it she will sleep as though unconscious and her parents, believing her dead, will take her to the Capulets' family vault. Romeo, summoned by Laurence, will return in secret to Verona and take her away with him to share his exile in Mantua.

Scene 3: Returning home, Juliet pretends to have submitted to her parent's wishes. The night before her marriage, Juliet is left alone in her room. She takes Laurence's potion and falls into a deep sleep.

Romeo and Juliet: Act. III Scene 1 with E. Gik-vaidze as Juliet and V. Smoltsov as Paris

In the morning, Juliet's friends appear together with the troubadours, Juliet's parents
and Paris. Not seeing Juliet in the room,
they are sure she is still sleeping. The musicians play merry music.

The girls and the youths dance. But still Juliet does not come out. The nurse looks behind the curtain and there is the « dead »
Juliet.

Scene 4: An autumn night in Mantua.
Romeo sits on a stone thinking of Juliet.

Romeo's faithful servant, Balthazzar, runs
in exhausted. He has reached Mantua before Laurence's messenger and tells Romeo
that Juliet is dead. The stricken Romeo
hurries to return to Verona.

Scene 5: A sad procession moves along the
path of the shadowy cemetery in Verona.

*Romeo and Juliet: Act. II Scene 3 with M. Gabovich
as Romeo*

Romeo and Juliet: Act. II Scene 3 with, S. Koren as Mercutio and A. Yermolaev as Tybalt

Romeo and Juliet: Galina Ulanova as Juliet and L. Zhdanov as Romeo

*Romeo and Juliet: Act. III Scene 1 with Galina
Ulanova as Juliet and V. Golubin as Paris*

Juliet's friends, her mother and father, her nurse and relations accompany the sleeping Juliet to the vault. As they mourn her death, the light fades and then, through the darkness, Romeo appears carrying a flaming torch. He bends over Juliet, admiring her beauty.

He takes poison and falls on the steps. Juliet wakes up and, seeing the dead Romeo, she tries to find the flask of poison so that she may drink the last drops herself. But it is empty. Taking Romeo's dagger,

she stabs herself. She has no use for life without Romeo.

Epilogue: The old Montague and Capulet come to the cemetery. They look on the dead bodies of their children and, overcome by the strength of their emotion, extend to each other the hand of reconciliation.

Romeo and Juliet: Act III Scene 5 with E. Gik-vaidze as Juliet and Y. Hofman as Romeo

Romeo and Juliet: Act. III Scene 5 with E. Gik-vaidze as Juliet and Y. Hofman as Romeo ▶

Don Quixote: Scene from Act. I, Sancho Panza is tossed in the air by the Merry-Makers

Don Quixote

Ballet in 4 Acts and 5 Scenes with a Prologue

MUSIC: Minkus

BOOK: M. Petipa. Didelot and Groski from story by Cervantes

CHOREOGRAPHY: M. Petipa

First Moscow performance at Bolshoi Theatre 14-12-1869 with A. Sobeshchanskaya as Kitri, Sokolov as Basil and I. Karpakova as Dulcinea

Prologue: In his ancestral house, Don Quixote reads a book and is inspired to go and find the fairy tale Princess Dulcinea, rescue her from disaster, fight for a cause and conquer the evil genius. He hires Sancho Panza —who has been caught by his servants stealing in the kitchen—to serve as his henchman. Don Quixote puts on his battered coat of mail, takes his useless pike and outmoded helmet and they set out.

Act I: The market place in Barcelona. The owner of the tavern wishes to marry his daughter, Kitri, to a rich nobleman, Camacho. This young fop is madly in love with Kitri but she has her own ideas about marriage. She loves the hairdresser, Basil, and tries to persuade her father that Basil is a better bridegroom for her. But in his opinion a barber is an unequal match for his daughter and, ignoring Basil, he welcomes Camacho as his guest in the tavern.

Kitri, flipping and flashing her yellow skirts and her scarlet fan, mimics her fop fiancé mischievously. Her friends, following her example, do everything they can to distract her father so that she and Basil can meet secretly.

The teasing and merry-making is at its height when Don Quixote and Sancho Panza ride into the square—the Don on an elderly horse and Sancho on a frightened little donkey. The townspeople are delighted with this strange couple and laugh at them frankly, although they are a little in awe of Don Quixote and his grand airs.

On seeing Kitri, Don Quixote takes her for Dulcinea, his fairy tale Princess, whom he has sworn to rescue from disaster.

Kitri and Basil decide to elope and, under the cover of the holiday merry-making, they run away. Her father, Camacho and Don Quixote go in search of her.

Act II: Kitri and Basil come to a tavern where Spanish dancers have assembled. Kitri's father and Camacho also arrive at the tavern in pursuit and the inn-keeper decides he will announce his daughter's engagement to Camacho immediately. But Basil, with Kitri's agreement, stages a scene of despair in which he pretends to stab himself with a dagger. Kitri cries over the body of her lover and Don Quixote, who has arrived full of noble indignation, accuses the inn-keeper of cruelty, and forces the worried father to agree to marry Kitri to the 'dying' Basil. The minute the father agrees and blesses them, Basil jumps up and everybody dances happily.

Scene 2: In his wanderings, Don Quixote arrives at a gypsy camp. The gypsies entertain him with a little stage show but he takes the misfortunes of the actors much too

Don Quixote: Decor for Act I (Model)

seriously and, forgetting that this is only a theatre, rushes to the stage to defend the oppressed and avenge the injured. He smashes up the entire stage, throws the villain about and then, catching sight of some windmills, near the gypsy encampment, he takes them for evil sorcerers and rushes to attack them with disastrous consequences.

*Don Quixote: Act I with O. Lepeshinskaya as Kitri
and A. Yermolaev as Basil*

Act III: Completely exhausted, Don Quixote and Sancho lie down to sleep in the forest. Don Quixote dreams—first a nightmare with everybody fighting him and then a beautiful sunny spring scene. He sees little cherubs and beautiful dryads—motionless ranks of ballerinas in pale pink and blue. In their leader, he thinks he recognises his Dulcinea and goes forward to meet her. (The Ballerina who plays the role of Kitri also dances this role in the dream sequence.)

Don Quixote wakes up again in the darkened forest. Sancho Panza is still sleeping but the sound of a hunting horn awakens him. A hunting party from a nearby castle comes through the forest. The Duke and Duchess are hunting ,attended by a magnificent suite. Sancho Panza appeals to them to rescue Don Quixote from his day-dreams. The Duke's

party, not averse to amusing themselves at the expense of the elderly knight-errant, invite him to their castle.

Act IV: The Duke's castle has been made ready for a pompous mock reception of Don Quixote. The Master of Ceremonies introduces Kitri and Basil who have been asked

Don Quixote: Act. 1 with A. Yermolaev as Basil and O. Lepeshinskaya as Kitri

*Don Quixote: Decor Act II Scene 2 (Model) - Below,
Decor Act II Scene 1 (Model)*

to play the roles of Dulcinea and an Unknown Knight.

Don Quixote and Sancho Panza are greeted and invited to places of honour and then a solemn procession begins with the « enchanted » Dulcinea passing by in a big chariot. Don Quixote goes up to her, eager to deliver her from the 'magic spell' but knows that, to achieve this, he must first fight the Unknown Knight. Basil, disguised in a helmet and visor, challenges Don Quixote to a duel and they both draw their swords.

But Don Quixote trips up over his spurs and falls. The Unknown Knight takes Dulcinea away. Basil throws off his disguise and they all dance joyfully, while the Duke and his suite laugh uproariously.

The ball continues while the lonely and melancholy Don Quixote, still loyal to his dreams, leaves together with Sancho Panza.

Don Quixote: Scene from Act III with Golovkina as Kitri

146

Don Quixote: Scene from Act III with O. Lepeshin-skaya as Kitri

Don Quixote: O. Lepeshinskaya as Kitri and A. Kuznetsov as Basil

Don Quixote: Scene from Act IV with M. Plisetskaya
as Kitri. Below, general view of Act IV

*Don Quixote: Act I. The market place in Barcelona
with Don Quixote on his old horse*

Don Quixote: Act IV with A. Yermolaev as Basil

Don Quixote: L. Cherkasova ▶

Cinderella: R. Struchkova as Cinderella and Y. Kon-dratov as the Prince

Cinderella

Ballet in 3 Acts

MUSIC: S. Prokofiev

BOOK: N. D. Volkov

CHOREOGRAPHY: R. Zakharov

First Moscow performance at Bolshoi Theatre 21-11-1945 with O. Lepeshinskaya as Cinderella and V. Preobrazhenski as the Prince

A richly furnished room in the house of Cinderella's father. Cinderella's stepmother and her two daughters have been invited to a court-ball and are now embroidering their shawls. By the fireplace is the ragged Cinderella. She has all the dirty jobs to do. The sisters sew the last stitches on their shawls and quarrel among themselves. Their mother puts an end to their quarrel by taking her two daughters out of the room. Cinderella, alone, recalls her childhood and those happy days when her mother was alive. Her father looks timidly in at the door. He wants to caress his daughter but is afraid that his shrewish and nagging wife will see him. Cinderella looks sadly at her father and he comes towards her but her stepmother, returning, throws herself angrily on her apologetic husband. Her daughters watch this domestic scene with satisfaction.

The fairy godmother appears, disguised as a beggarwoman. Nobody recognises her as she begs for alms and Cinderella's stepmother turns her out of the house. But Cinderella gives the old woman her own supper—a piece of bread. The fairy godmother looks at the kind-hearted girl affectionately and vanishes, as mysteriously as she appeared.

A motley troupe of tradesmen burst into the room: tailors and seamstresses, a hairdresser and a jeweller. There is a gay commotion in the house as the daughters and their mother dress for the ball. A dancing teacher and a violinist are also in the room for a rehearsal of the gavotte before the ball. The teacher is displeased with the silly sisters. Hiding in a corner, the wistful Cinderella watches the preparations. She, too, would like to go to the ball but it is no place for a drudge. The stepmother, the sisters and the father, loaded down with their bits and pieces, set off for the palace. Cinderella dreams of the ball. She imagines a handsome young man coming to meet her and dances around with him in a waltz, pretending the broom she holds is he. After the waltz, she dances the gavotte which her sisters had just been practising.

The fairy godmother appears once again. She gives the young girl some beautiful slippers and summons the four seasons of the year to dress Cinderella for the ball.

One after the other, the fairies appear with their suites—Spring, Summer, Autumn and Winter. Spring brings flowers; Summer, a lovely dress; Autumn, a brocade cloak; Winter, diamonds.

All is ready for the ball but the fairy godmother points to the clock and warns Cinderella that she must leave the ball at midnight otherwise the magic spell will be broken.

A waltz is played for her departure and, accompanied by the stars, Cinderella goes off to the ball.

Cinderella: Act. I with R. Struchkova as Cinderella, V. Krieger as the Stepmother and N. Gerber as Cinderella's father

156

Act II: A luxurious room in the palace. The ball has started but the Prince has not yet arrived. The courtiers perform a stately dance.

Cinderella's family arrives.

The sisters being rich heiresses, several poor noblemen would be very willing to gild their coats of arms with their dowries and two courtiers, in search of rich wives, begin

Cinderella: Act I with R. Struchkova as Cinderella and G. Petrova as the Fairy Godmother

to flirt with the sisters. Just as a mazurka begins, the gallant young Prince, bursts into the room like a whirlwind and sits on the throne like a horseman in the saddle.

The court jester capers before the throne. The mazurka, interrupted by the entrance of the Prince, begins again and the Prince

Cinderella: Galina Ulanova as Cinderella and V. Ryadshev as Cinderella's father

reluctantly joins the dancers. He dances with the sisters who vainly attempt to win his affection. There is the sound of fairy music and everyone looks towards the entrance.

First the stars enter and then Cinderella herself, looking so beautiful that all take her for a princess.

The young Prince is captivated by Cinderella's beauty and the stepmother and sisters do not recognise her.

Three girls and a negro bring Cinderella three oranges—rare fruits in the Prince's country, but the stepmother and the sisters snatch the oranges. The room gradually empties and the Prince and Cinderella, left alone, declare their love for each other. The

Cinderella: Decor for Act II (Model)

waltz begins again and, dancing with the Prince, Cinderella forgets the fairy's warning. The threatening sound of the clock's tick is heard and then midnight strikes. Cinderella flees from the palace, leaving behind a slipper. The Prince and his guests search for the missing princess in dismay. The Prince picks up the slipper. He has now only one thought—to find his beloved princess—the owner of the little slipper.

Act III: The night after the ball. All the shoemakers of the town have assembled before the distracted Prince. None of them has ever made so lovely a slipper. The Prince, seizing the slipper, jumps through the window and sets off in search of Cinderella even though he may have to travel the world. In his travels, the Prince comes first to Andalusia, then the east—but nowhere can he find a maiden whose foot fits the lost slipper.

Once again he returns to his own town.

While the Prince was travelling in foreign lands, night has changed to day and Cinderella in her old rags has woken up at home in her place by the fireside. Was it a dream? But, taking from her apron the little slipper which she has hidden there, she convinces herself that she really was in a palace and danced with the Prince. The sisters hurry

Cinderella: Act II Scene 2 with B. Galetskaya as the Andalusian girl and G. Tarabanov as the Andalusian youth

in to tell Cinderella about their success at the ball, show her the oranges and finally quarrel between themselves again.

From the street there is noise and confusion. Friends, rushing in, tell them the Prince is looking everywhere for the girl who has lost her slipper. The Prince enters and the trying on of the slipper begins. The sisters and the stepmother try in vain to put on the tiny shoe. Cinderella, on her knees, helps them and, as she does, the hidden slipper falls

Cinderella: Act II with R. Struchkova as Cinderella

out of her apron. The Prince sees the second slipper and, in the modest Cinderella, he recognises the fairy princess of the ball.

The fairy godmother enters and brings the lovers together.

In a beautiful garden, among fairies and stars, the Prince and Cinderella begin their happy life together.

Cinderella: R. Struchkova as Cinderella

Cinderella: Act II with R. Struchkova as Cinderella

Cinderella: Y. Gerber as the Jester

Cinderella: Act III with Galina Ulanova as Cinderella and V. Preobrashenski as the Prince

Cinderella: Galina Ulanova as Cinderella and V.
Preobrazhenski as the Prince (above and opposite)

*Giselle : Act II Galina Ulanova as Giselle and V.
Preobrazhenski as Albrecht*

Giselle

Ballet in 2 Acts

MUSIC: A. Adam

BOOK: T. Gautier and Saint-Georges

CHOREOGRAPHY: Coralli

First Moscow performance at Bolshoi Theatre 25-11-1843 with E. Andreyanova as Giselle

The young peasant girl, Giselle, loves and is loved in return. She does not know that her lover is the Count Albrecht in disguise. She never questions him but runs joyfully out of her house whenever he calls to her through the window... although her mother tries to restrain Giselle from frolicking with the village maidens as she has a weak heart.

During a hunt in a neighbouring part of their estate, Albrecht's father, with Albrecht's fiancee and his retinue, stops for a rest in Giselle's village. These noble ladies and gentlemen are unbelievably magnificent. Dressed in orange, scarlet, white and cloth of gold, they entrance Giselle who, in her simple, sheltered life, has never seen such grandeur. She is particularly attracted to Albrecht's fiancee, who is touched by the young peasant girl's naive charm and gives Giselle a string of beads she is wearing. A woodcutter, who is in love with Giselle and wishes to expose the Count who has deceived her, reveals Albrecht's secret. At first Giselle will not believe him. But when Albrecht is brought on to the stage and confronted with his fiancee, Giselle throws the string of beads on the ground, loses her reason, has a heart attack and dies.

Act II: There is a legend that jilted maidens who die before their marriages rise from their graves at night and lead wanderers in a giddy dance to death. The scene opens by Giselle's grave. Magic blue lights twinkle among the trees, ushering in the Willis, who glide through trap-doors, lean from ivy-hung branches or float through space. The Queen of the Willis, Myrta, welcomes Giselle to their ghostly gathering.

Their first victim is the woodcutter. He has come to Giselle's grave, tormented by pangs of conscience, and the Willis dance with him until he falls exhausted on the ground.

The woodcutter is followed by Albrecht, now stricken with remorse. The same fate that befell the woodcutter now awaits him. Giselle tries to intercede for Albrecht but Myrta will not listen. The Bacchanalia of the Willis works up to a climax. Giselle again comes to protect Albrecht. He is already weak and powerless when a church bell sounds, heralding the dawn. The Willis fade into the night and the sun's first beams illumine the kneeling figure of Albrecht. Giselle's love has saved him from death.

Giselle: P. Adrianov

Giselle: Act I. Galina Ulanova as Giselle ▶

Giselle: Act I. R. Struchkova as Giselle

Giselle: Act II. V. Preobrazhenski as Albrecht

Giselle: A. Yermolaev as Albrecht

Giselle: Act. II with Galina Ulanova as Giselle and V. Preobrazhenski as Albrecht. ▶

*Giselle: Act I with Galina Ulanova as Giselle and
M. Gabovich as Albrecht*

Giselle: Yuri Zhdanov as Albrecht

Shurale Act II. M. Plisetskaya as the Bird-maiden

Shurale

Ballet in 3 Acts

MUSIC: F. Yarullin

BOOK: A. Faize and L. Jacobson based on Tartar folk tales

CHOREOGRAPHY: L. Jacobson

First Moscow performance at Bolshoi Theatre 29-1-1955 with M. Plisetskaya as the Bird-maiden, Y. Kondratov as Batyr

Night in the depths of a wood. The white lights of the moon can scarcely be seen through the overhanging clouds. The sinister shapes of age-old trees point their twisted branches to the sky. Here, in the heart of the wood, in the hollow of an immense withered tree, lives Shurale, the sovereign of the dense forest.

A young man, Batyr, comes out into a clearing in the wood. Noticing a bird flying past, Batyr shoots at it from his bow and, rushing off, is soon hidden by the thickets.

Suddenly, one of the branches of a vast oak tree comes to life. This is not a branch, it is Shurale himself. He comes out into the clearing with his eyes blazing like coals. His long claws are ready to seize his prey. All the evil spirits of the forest, who are subservient to Shurale, awake. Witches, evil genies, gnomes and goblins entertain their lord with dances. But, as the sun rises, only Shurale and the goblins are left in the clearing.

The sun rises still higher. A flock of birds flies over the awakening wood. They alight in the green clearing, throw off their wings and, turning into maidens, run off into the wood. Only one bird remains in the clearing. She circles round gaily, not noticing Shurale hidden behind a tree. Finally, she too throws off her wings, turns into a beautiful girl and also hides in the wood.

With an evil leer, Shurale creeps over to the wings, steals them and takes them off into his den.

The girls come out of the wood, caressed by the freshness of the sun and the morning and begin to play games in the clearing. Suddenly Shurale, jumping down from a tree, rushes towards them. The frightened girls hasten to put on their wings and, turning themselves into birds again, fly off.

Only one girl is left in the clearing. She cannot find her wings. Rushing about in despair, she stares up at her friends who are flying further and further away. Then suddenly Shurale appears before her. The girl wants to escape but Shurale bars the way. The goblins, obeying their master, surround her from all sides and Shurale revels in his prisoner's terror. Then, chasing the goblins away, he reaches towards the bird-maiden, already rejoicing in his victory. But Batyr runs in from the wood and, seeing Shurale advancing on the bird-maiden, rushes to her assistance. Shurale jumps in fury on to Batyr's shoulders and tries to strangle him but Batyr throws Shurale to the ground. The defeated Shurale falls at the foot of an old tree.

Helped by Batyr, the bird-maiden looks for her wings again but she cannot find them. In despair, she sinks down on to the grass and cries bitterly. Tormented by terror and in tears, she falls asleep and Batyr stands

for a long time over the sleeping bird-maiden, struck by her super-human beauty. Then he carefully lifts her in his arms and leaves the wood with his precious burden. Shurale recovers consciousness and, with his host of evil spirits, threatens Batyr, who is carrying off the bird-maiden, with a dreadful fate.

Shurale: Scene from Act II. The courtyard of Batyr's house

Shurale: Scene from Act II. The guests try to hide the Bird-maiden (Plisetskaya) from Batyr

Shurale: Act. II with M. Plisetskaya as the Bird-maiden and Y. Kondratov as Batyr

Act II: The sun shines brightly over the gaily festooned courtyard of Batyr's house. The whole village has gathered for the betrothal of Batyr and the bird-maiden. Young and old make merry and children run happily among the guests. The matchmakers come into the courtyard and, in accordance with the Tartar custom, ask the groom to find his bride. But however much the guests try to hide her, Batyr succeeds in finding his fiancée among her new friends.

The old folk solemnly announce the betrothal of Batyr and his beautiful bird-maiden. But her thoughts are far away and she pines for her lost wings. In order to distract his fiancée from her sad thoughts, Batyr calls to his friends and starts a wild dance. There

Shurale: Act II with M. Plisetskaya as the Bird-maiden

seems to be no end to the merrymaking but the bird-maiden remains sad.

Night falls and the merrymakers disperse. Nobody has noticed that Shurale has entered Batyr's courtyard. Hiding in dark corners, frightening the matchmakers and jumping out unexpectedly to tease the guests, Shurale chooses a moment when the melancholy bird-maiden is alone and then throws her wings into the courtyard.

Seeing her wings, the bird-maiden, trembling with joy, presses them to her heart. She wants to fly away but pauses doubtfully as she does not want to leave Batyr. However her desire to fly up into the heavenly heights overcomes her love for her betrothed. Throwing a last farewell glance towards the house which has now become so dear to her, she soars up into the sky.

At a sign from Shurale, she is surrounded by a flock of black crows. The bird tries to free herself but the crows, forming a tight circle around her, carry her off. The triumphant Shurale rushes after them.

The terrified guests call Batyr. He runs out into the courtyard and sees the black flock flying away high into the sky and, among them, a beautiful white bird flapping its wings.

Seizing a torch, Batyr rushes out of the courtyard and disappears into the darkness of the night.

Shurale: Scene from Act II. The courtyard of Batyr's house.

184

Act III: Shurale's sinister lair. The bird-maiden is here again, the terrified prisoner of the ruler of the deep forests. In vain does Shurale try to overcome the bird-maiden's resistance. She takes no notice of him. From all sides the dark denizens of the forest gather round on Shurale's summons.

The bird-maiden hates the evil ruler of the woods. Shurale's anger rises and he rushes towards the girl and lifts her up to throw her to the baying pack of evil spirits who are waiting to tear her to pieces. But, at this moment, a crow suddenly flies into the clearing and warns Shurale of Batyr's approach. Then Batyr rushes into the clearing with the torch in his hand.

Shurale: Scene from Act II with Y. Kondratov as Batyr in the centre

Shurale, the gnomes and the witches rush at the youth in fury while the goblins try to hide the bird-maiden. But Batyr, in a life and death struggle, snatches the bird-maiden from their claws and sets fire to the wood in an attempt to destroy the evil spirits. Tongues of flame envelop Shurale's kingdom. The burning gnomes and witches rush about in terror amid the flaming trees. Gathering together all his remaining strength, Batyr pushes Shurale into the fire. In a moment the flames turn the evil ruler of the woods into ashes.

A sea of fire is all around. Batyr gives the bird-maiden her wings and begs her to fly out of the wood, leaving him to perish alone in the fire. But she will not leave Batyr. Realising that her love for him is stronger than her desire to live and to fly away, she hurls her wings into the flames. This act of love and courage is immediately rewarded and the forest fire is extinguished as though it had never been.

The sun rises, pouring its bright rays onto

the golden leaves. A flock of birds alights in the clearing. They have flown here to say a last farewell to their friend. Then the matchmakers, the relations and the friends of Batyr also come into the wood which has now been freed from the evil spirits. They all surround the betrothed couple, wishing them happiness and joy.

Shurale: Act II with M. Plisetskaya as the Bird-maiden

Shurale: Act II with M. Plisetskaya as the Bird-maiden and Y. Kondratov as Batyr

Shurale: Scene from Act III. Shurale's sinister lair, with V. Lebashev as Shurale

Shurale: M. Plisetskaya as the Bird-maiden, Y. Kondratov as Batyr and V. Lebashev as Shurale ▶

Laurencia: Act. I, The village of Fuenteovejuna,
with M. Plisetskaya as Laurencia

Laurencia

Ballet in 3 Acts and 6 Scenes

MUSIC: A. Krein

BOOK: E. Mandelberg after « Fuente Ovéjuna » of Lopé de Vega

CHOREOGRAPHY: V. M. Chaboukiani

First Moscow performance at Bolshoi Theatre 1956 with M. Plisetskaya as Laurencia and Y. Kondratov as Frondozo

Spain at the end of the XVth century The Village of Fuenteovejuna. The peasants are returning from the fields. The young people sit down in the village square to rest. The mischievous Pascuala enters with her companions and also Laurencia, daughter of the village elder Estevan, with the village youths contending for her favours. Among them is Frondozo. He has long been in love with Laurencia, but the proud beauty passes by without so much as noticing him.

The strolling musician Mengo arrives and the girls beg him to play. How can he refuse when Pascuala joins her plea to those of the rest? Frondozo declares his love to Laurencia only to be rebuffed once more.

A trumpet sounds—the Lord of the Village is returning home from a compaign. The old men, led by Estevan, go out to meet him. Flores and Ortuno, his retainers, jostle the crowd to clear a way for their master. In comes Don Fernan Gomez de Guzman, Lord of the Village. Estevan brings him a glass of wine and congratulates him on his victorious campaign. The girls, with Laurencia at their head, approach timidly and lay bouquets of flowers at Don Fernan's feet.

Don Fernan notices Laurencia, and tries to approach her, but her friends gather round to protect her. He orders Flores and Ortuno to clear away the peasants. Only Laurencia and Pascuala remain on the square and Don Fernan invites them into his castle. But they refuse. He orders Flores and Ortuno to bring them, but Mengo comes to the rescue and they escape and run away.

Scene 2: By the river near the village. Down the hill comes Laurencia with a basket of washing on her arm. Frondozo arrives and makes her yet another declaration of love but she is pitiless, and merely laughs at his despair. He goes away.

From the wood appears Don Fernan, out hunting, with a cross-bow in his hand. Delighted to find Laurencia, he offers her rich gifts but she pushes them scornfully aside. Blinded by passion, he catches her in his arms. At this moment Frondozo returns and, seizing Don Fernan's bow, threatens to shoot. Don Fernan is forced to release the girl and she flees. Frondozo disappears into the thicket pursued by Don Fernan.

Pascuala and her friends enter with their

baskets of washing. Seeing Mengo approach, the girls hide in the wood and pelt him with fir-cones, wherupon Mengo makes as though to steal their baskets. This soon brings them out of their hiding place.

Jacinta comes rushing out of the wood in fright pursued by Don Fernan's men. The girls run off in all directions and Mengo attempts to defend Jacinta. But the soldiers knock him down and Don Fernan appears.

Jacinta and Mengo beg him to let them go, but the tyrant, maddened by the peasant's

Laurencia: Decor for Act I. The village of Fuenteovejuna

impertinence, hands them over to the mercy of the soldiers.

Anxious' about the fate of Frondozo, Laurencia returns to the river bank with a crowd of peasants. Mengo staggers out of the wood and Laurencia is about to rush towards him when Frondozo reappears. No longer able to conceal her love for him, she throws her

192

Laurencia: Scene from Act III with M. Plisetskaya in foreground

Laurencia: Act I with M. Plisetskaya as Laurencia

Laurencia: Scene from Act II with H. Kapustina in the centre

Laurencia: Scene from Act II. The village square. Estevan offers Don Fernan a goblet of wine, M. Plisetskaya and Y. Kondratov on the right

Laurencia: Scene from Act II. Left to right, R. Struchkova and P. Andrianov, M. Plisetskaya and Y. Kondratov, M. Gotlieb and G. Evdokimov

arms round the youth's neck. He is delighted. Estevan gives Laurencia and Frondozo
his blessing.

Jacinta appears and tells the peasants of
Fuenteovejuna of the violence she has suffe-
red at the hands of Don Fernan's men.

Act III: The village square. The whole
population of the village is assembled round
the festive board. A band of gypsies arrives—
guests from a nearby encampment. The
bridal couple, Laurencia and Frondozo,
return from church. Estevan and Juan,
Frondozo's father, start the dancing.

Laurencia: Act III with A. Lapauri as Don Fernan.
Dances with his friends, V. Faerfax and G. Kuznet-
zova.

Jacinta alone is sad, feeling her sorrow all
the more bitterly for seeing the happy bridal
pair. Mengo consoles her.

Don Fernan and his soldiers arrive unexpectedly on the square. Estevan offers Don
Fernan a goblet of wine but the tyrant,
catching sight of Laurencia and Frondozo
clad in wedding garb, smashes the goblet

furiously to the ground and orders his soldiers to seize the bridal pair.

The old men plead in vain but Don Fernan will not relent. Estevan, as a protest, hands over his staff of office. Don Fernan seizes it and strikes him with it.

Laurencia and Frondozo are led away by the soldiers.

Estevan, in despair, picks up his daughter's wedding veil and the peasants gather round him, clenching their fists in fury.

Act III: Night. The park in front of Don Fernan's castle. In the shadow of the trees,

Laurencia: Scene from Act III with M. Plisetskaya as Laurencia

surrounding the castle, crouch the peasants. Suddenly the gates of the castle are thrown open, Flores and Ortuno push out Laurencia, wretched and bedraggled. She staggers blindly forward, and her eye suddenly falls on her father, Mengo and all the peasants from her village. She looks at them with contempt. They should be ashamed of themselves, she says, for permitting such a fate to befall her. Her grief is the last drop in the bitter cup of the people's suffering. Led by Laurencia, the villagers of Fuenteovejuna storm Don Fernan's castle.

Scene 2: Inside the castle. Don Fernan and his friends are making merry. Flores and Ortuno rush in to tell him that the peasants, in revolt, are approaching the castle. Don Fernan merely laughs at the fears of his men. He orders Frondozo to be brought in and taunts the helpless youth.

The noise of the peasants' uprising draws nearer and nearer. They break into the

Laurencia: Decor for Act III Scene 2. Inside the castle of Don Fernan

castle. Hoping to save his skin, Don Fernan offers them a casket of gold but the people, with one accord, condemn him to death. The peasants kill Don Fernan and set fire to the castle.

Scene 3: In front of the blazing castle, the villagers celebrate their victory.

*Red Sails: I. Tikhomirnova as Asol and V. Preo-
brazhenski as Grey*

Red Sails

Ballet in 3 Acts and 5 Scenes with Prologue and Epilogue

MUSIC: V. Yurovski

BOOK: A. Talanov from a story by A. Green

CHOREOGRAPHY: A. I. Radunski, L. Pospekhin and N. M. Popko

First performance at Kuibishev during evacuation from Moscow of the Bolshoi Company 30-12-1942 with I. Tikhomirnova as Asol, V. Preobrazhenski as Grey and A. Radunski as Egl

Prologue: Night. A storm rages at sea. On the shore a group of women and old men are anxiously awaiting the return of the fishermen.

A boat draws in to shore, and a young fisherman steps out. It is Grey. All eyes turn towards him, and in all he reads the same question: « What is happening, out there at sea? » Grey consoles the distraught women.

Out of the raging seas a large boat looms in sight, and Grey helps it to beach. Limp and exhausted, the fishermen stumble out. Weeping with joy, their wives and mothers embrace them and lead them home. Grey helps one of the men, wounded in the leg, back to his hut.

Alone on the deserted shore remains Anna. Her husband, Langren, has still not returned and, clutching her little daughter Asol, she gazes anxiously out towards the horizon, seeing in every log cast up by the waves a boat bringing her husband back and in every scrap of driftwood tossed by the breakers a human hand appealing for help. Utterly exhausted, she weeps disconsolately.

Anna is watched by Menners, the storekeeper, who has come down to the beach in search of loot washed up by the storm. An evil, greedy fellow, he has long coveted Anna and now, seeing her wrapped in loneliness and grief, he seizes the opportunity to embrace her. Anna struggles in vain to escape from his persistent advances but Grey arrives, and chases Menners away.

Far out at sea, a black speck becomes visible. Langren's boat! But the tempestuous wind drives it on to the sheer rocks. Lashing a rope to his waist, Grey plunges boldly into the sea, soon to return bringing Langren. Anna rushes fainting into her husband's arms. Grey helps to carry her back home and departs. Little Asol gazes long after her father's rescuer.

Act I: Anna has died and Langren has taken to earning a livelihood by carving little toy boats which he takes to the market to sell. Asol sits in the doorway helping her father fit the boats with sails. Langren gives her one for herself. She clutches it delightedly to her breast.

Langren goes off to the market, Asol waves him goodbye and then returns to take her boat down to the sea to sail. It is snatched up by the wind, and carried far to sea. Asol tries to rush after it but her way is barred by Menners, the storekeeper's son, sauntering along the shore with his friends—rich men's sons and gaudily dressed girls. The boys lash at Asol with their long switches, laughing with glee at her attempts to escape. A boat draws in to shore, bringing Egl, a wandering musician, and Grey who chase young Menners and his gang away. Grey, to console the little girl, tears his red kerchief into strips and deftly turns it into little red sails for her toy boat.

Asol stares spellbound at the red-sailed boat and at Grey smiling down at her.

« Just you wait, Asol, I shall become a captain and sail real ships and I shall rig up my ship with red sails just like these, and come and take you away from Menners and his gang », Grey tells the girl.

Asol clutches her boat tenderly in her arms. In her imagination she already sees Grey's stately ship, with real red sails gleaming in the sun.

Act II: Several years have gone by. Langren has become a sailor again and is off to sea. Henceforth Asol will have to take the toy ships to market. At the edge of the wood, Langren bids his daughter farewell.

The forest is filled with the soft rustling of the pines. Asol sits down to rest, holding in her hands the little toy boat with the red sails which she carries with her wherever she goes. Suddenly she falls asleep and, once again, she dreams—as she has dreamt so many times before—of the beautiful red-sailed ship floating over the waves with Grey at the helm. Grey comes towards her with outstretched arms, Asol gazes tenderly into his eyes—and wakes up. It was only a dream, whispered into her ear by the tall, stately pines.

Scene 2: Three years later a ship sails into port returning from a distant voyage. At the helm is Grey. Bold and fearless, he has attained his goal. He has become the most skilled of all the captains in the port. The people joyfully welcome the sailors home. There are men from all over the world in the happy crew—local boys, a negro from the banks of the Zambezi river, a Malay from the sunny archipelago, a lad from distant China...

The sailors come ashore and begin to dance. Merry Letika and his betrothed, sailors and their girls, dance with joy for the ship has come home. Egl is there, an old friend of Grey's, the charcoal burners and the town gentry. Menners and his friends and the dolled-up girls dance on their own until they are driven away by the mockery of the crowd. Gradually the merry-makers disperse. The square becomes deserted.

On to the jetty comes Asol, hurrying to Menner's shop, with her weekly batch of toys. In answer to her knock, Menners comes out drunk and snarls that her last lot of toys is still unsold, and he wants no more from her. Snatching the tray from her arms, he casts it down to the ground, shattering the boats to splinters. Poor Asol is in despair. Grey and Egl enter the square. Grey's heart leaps for joy when he sees Asol. He is about to rush up to her, but Egl holds him back. « You see the boat Asol is holding so tenderly? », he says. « She never lets it out of her sight, and she believes that you are coming one day in a real red-sailed ship to take her away. »

Grey creeps up to Asol, takes the boat when she is not looking and, taking the ring off his finger, slips it on to hers. He and Egl go out. Looking back, they see Asol searching anxiously for her boat.

Suddenly she notices the ring on her finger, and stares in amazement.

« What is it, and where has it come from? » There is no one in sight. Then suddenly a thought flashes through her mind... can it be a sign that Grey will come soon to fetch her?

Asol goes out confused but with sparkling eyes. Grey gazes lovingly after her, holding in his hand the little red-sailed ship.

He resolves to make the fairy tale told to Asol so long ago come true. « Wait for me, Asol! Soon I shall come for you, as I promised, in a majestic red-sailed ship, » he says as he watches girl fading into the distance.

Act III: Early morning. Asol is sitting on the seashore. Ever since the day when the little toy ship disappeared, she has been dreaming and dreaming of Grey. Yet still he does not come.

Along come Asol's friends, the charcoal burners, calling to her and pointing out to sea. Asol gazes into the distance and turns away afraid to believe her own eyes. But no, it is not a dream.

Riding proudly on the crest of the waves, a ship draws into shore, red sails swelling in the breeze. Asol stretches out her arms. How long she has waited and believed that he would come, and now he is here!

Scene 2: Grey's ship is gaily beflagged and the sailors hold bunches of flowers. At a sign from the signaller, the hubbub dies down. Asol comes up on deck and, seeing Grey, goes slowly up to him, points to the ring on her finger. — « Is this yours? » He nods his head. « Yes ».

The silence is broken by Letika, who orders casks of wine to be brought up from the hold. Glasses fill up and Letika, to the accompaniment of a burst of music, begins to dance. The dancers follow each other thick and fast in the shadow of the red sail. Suddenly a trumpet sounds. The sailors rush to the side of the ship—it is the boat sent to fetch Langren. They help the old man aboard.

Langren is lost in amazement. All his life he has sailed the seven seas but never has he set eyes on a ship as beautiful as this. Asol and Grey approach, and ask his blessing. The old man joins their hands together. The ship weighs anchor and, red sails billowing in the wind, sets off on a long and happy voyage.

Epilogue: Egl waves farewell to the red-sailed ship as it fades away into the distance.

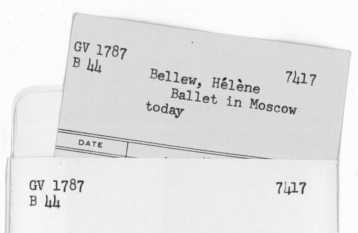